The Voice of the Pack

By Edison Marshall

PROLOGUE

If one can just lie close enough to the breast of the wilderness, he can't help but be imbued with some of the life that pulses therein.--From a Frontiersman's Diary.

Long ago, when the great city of Gitcheapolis was a rather small, untidy hamlet in the middle of a plain, it used to be that a pool of water, possibly two hundred feet square, gathered every spring immediately back of the courthouse. The snow falls thick and heavy in Gitcheapolis in winter; and the pond was nothing more than snow water that the inefficient drainage system of the city did not quite absorb. Now snow water is occasionally the most limpid, melted-crystal thing in the world. There are places just two thousand miles west of Gitcheapolis where you can see it pouring pure and fresh off of the snow fields, scouring out a ravine from the great rock wall of a mountain side, leaping faster than a deer leaps--and when you speak of the speed of a descending deer you speak of something the usual mortal eye can scarcely follow--from cataract to cataract; and the sight is always a pleasing one to behold. Incidentally, these same snow streams are quite often simply swarming with trout,--brook and cutthroat, steelhead and even those speckled fellows that fishermen call Dolly Vardens for some reason that no one has ever quite been able to make out. They are to be found in every ripple, and they bite at a fly as if they were going to crush the steel hook into dust between their teeth, and the cold water gives them spirit to fight until the last breath of strength is gone from their beautiful bodies. How they came there, and what their purpose is in ever climbing up the river that leads nowhere but to a snow bank, no one exactly knows.

The snow water back of the courthouse was not like this at all. Besides being the despair of the plumber and the city engineer, it was a severe strain on the beauty-loving instincts of every inhabitant in the town who had any such instincts. It was muddy and murky and generally distasteful; and lastly, there were no trout in it. Neither were there any mud cat such as were occasionally to be caught in the Gitcheapolis River.

A little boy played at the edge of the water, this spring day of long ago. Except for his interest in the pond, it would have been scarcely worth while to go to the trouble of explaining that it contained no fish. He, however, bitterly regretted the fact. In truth, he sometimes liked to believe that it did contain fish, very sleepy fish that never made a ripple, and as he had an uncommon imagination he was sometimes able to convince himself that this was so. But he never took hook and line and played at fishing. He was too much afraid of the laughter of his boy friends. His mother probably wouldn't object if he fished here, he thought, particularly if he were careful not to get his shoes covered with mud. But she wouldn't let him go down to Gitcheapolis Creek to fish with the other boys for mud cat. He was not very strong, she thought, and it was a rough sport anyway, and besides,--she didn't think he wanted to go very badly. As mothers are usually particularly understanding, this was a curious thing.

The truth was that little Dan Failing wanted to fish almost as much as he wanted to live. He would dream about it of nights. His blood would glow with the thought of it in the springtime. Women the world over will have a hard time believing what an intense, heart-devouring passion the love of the chase can be, whether it is for fishing or hunting or merely knocking golf balls into a little hole upon a green. Sometimes they don't remember that this instinct is just as much a part of most men, and thus most boys, as their hands or their lips. It was acquired by just as laborious a process,--the lives of uncounted thousands of ancestors who fished and hunted for a living.

It was true that little Dan didn't look the part. Even then he showed signs of physical frailty. His eyes looked rather large, and his cheeks were not the color of fresh sirloin as they should have been. In fact, one would have had to look very hard to see any color in them at all. These facts are interesting from the light they throw upon the next glimpse of Dan, fully twenty years later.

This story isn't about the pool of snow water; it is only partly about Gitcheapolis. "Gitche" means great in the Indian language, and every one knows what "apolis" means. There are a dozen cities in the middle-western part of the United States just like it--with Indian names, with muddy, snow-water pools, with slow rivers in which only mud cat live--utterly surrounded by endless fields that slope levelly and evenly to a drab horizon. And because that land is what it is, because there are such cities as Gitcheapolis, there has sprung up in this decade a farseeing breed of men.

They couldn't help but learn to see far, on such prairies. And, like little Dan by the pool, they did all their hunting and their fishing and exercised many of the instincts that a thousand generations of wild men had instilled in them, in their dreams alone. It was great exercise for the imagination. And perhaps that has had something to do with the size of the crop of writers and poets and artists that is now being harvested in the Middle West.

Except for the fact that it was the background for the earliest picture of little Dan, the pool back of the courthouse has very little importance in his story. It did, however, afford an illustration to him of one of the really astonishing truths of life. He saw a shadow in the water that he pretended he thought might be a fish. He threw a stone at it.

The only thing that happened was a splash, and then a slowly widening ripple. The circumference of the ripple grew ever larger, extended and widened, and finally died at the edge of the shore. It set little Dan to thinking. He wondered if, had the pool been larger, the ripple still would have spread; and if the pool had been eternity, whether the ripple would have gone on forever. At the time he did not know the laws of cause and effect. Later, when Gitcheapolis was great and prosperous and no longer untidy, he was going to find out that a cause is nothing but a rock thrown into a pond of infinity, and the ripple that is its effect keeps growing and growing forever.

It is a very old theme, but the astonishment it creates is always new. A man once figured out that if Clovis had spared one life that he took--say that of the under-chief whose skull he shattered to pay him for breaking the vase of Soissons--there would be to-day the same races but an entirely different set of individuals. The effect would grow and grow as the years passed. The man's progeny each in turn would leave his mark upon the world, and the result would be--too vast to contemplate. The little incident that is the real beginning of this story was of no more importance than a pebble thrown into the snow-water pond; but its effect was to remove the life of Dan Failing, since grown up, far out of the realms of the ordinary.

And that brings all matters down to 1919, in the last days of a particularly sleepy summer. You would hardly know Gitcheapolis now. It is true that the snows still fall deep in winter, but the city engineer has finally solved the problem of the pool back of the courthouse. In fact, the courthouse itself is gone, and rebuilt in a more pretentious section of the city. The business district has increased tenfold. And the place where used to be the pool and the playground of Dan Failing is now laid off in as green and pretty a city park as one could wish to see.

The evidence points to the conclusion that the story some of the oldest settlers told about this district was really so. They say that forty and fifty and maybe seventy-five years ago, the quarter-section where the park was laid out was a green little glade, with a real, natural lake in the center. Later the lake was drained to raise com, and the fish therein--many of them such noble fish as perch and bass--all died in the sun-baked mud. The pool that had gathered yearly was just the lake trying, like a spent prize fighter, to come back. And it is rather singular that buildings have been torn down and money has been spent to restore the little glade to its original charm; and now construction has been started to build an artificial lake in the center. One would be inclined to wonder why things weren't kept the way they were in the first place. But that is the way of cities.

Some day, when the city becomes more prosperous, a pair of swans and a herd of deer are going to be introduced, to restore some of the natural wild life of the park. But in the summer of 1919, a few small birds and possibly half a dozen pairs of squirrels were the extent and limit of the wild creatures. And at the moment this story opens, one of these squirrels was perched on a wide-spreading limb overarching a gravel path that slanted through the sunlit park. The squirrel was hungry. He wished that some one would come along with a nut.

There was a bench beneath the tree. If there had not been, the life of Dan Failing would have been entirely different. In fact, as the events will show, there wouldn't have been any life worth talking about at all. If the squirrel had been on any other tree, if he hadn't been hungry, if any one of a dozen other things hadn't been as they were, Dan Failing would have never gone back to the land of his people. The little bushy-tailed fellow on the tree limb was the squirrel of Destiny!

BOOK ONE

REPATRIATION

Dan Failing stepped out of the elevator and was at once absorbed in the crowd that ever surged up and down Broad Street. Where the crowd came from, or what it was doing, or where it was going was one of the mysteries of Gitcheapolis. It appealed to a person rather as does a river: eternal, infinite, having no control over its direction or movement, but only subject to vast, underlying natural laws. In this case, the laws were neither gravity nor cohesion, but rather unnamed laws that go clear back to the struggle for existence and self-preservation. Once in the crowd, Failing surrendered up all individuality. He was just one of the ordinary drops of water, not an interesting, elaborate, physical and chemical combination to be studied on the slide of a microscope. No one glanced at him in particular. He was enough like the other drops of water not to attract attention. He wore fairly passable clothes, neither rich nor shabby. He was a tall man, but gave no impression of strength because of the exceeding spareness of his frame. As long as he remained in the crowd, he wasn't important enough to be studied. But soon he turned off, through the park, and straightway found himself alone.

The noise and bustle of the crowd--never loud or startling, but so continuous that the senses are scarcely more aware of them than of the beating of one's own heart--suddenly and utterly died almost at the very border of the park. It was as if an ax had chopped them off, and left the silence of the wild place. The gravel path that slanted through the green lawns did not lead anywhere in particular. It made a big loop and came out almost where it went in. Perhaps that is the reason that the busy crowds did not launch forth upon it. Crowds, like electricity, take the shortest course. Moreover, the hour was still some distance from noon, and the afternoon pleasure seekers had not yet come. But the morning had advanced far enough so that all the old castaways that had slept in the park had departed. Dan had the path all to himself.

Although he had plenty of other things to think about, the phenomena of the sudden silence came home to him very straight indeed. The noise from the street seemed wholly unable to penetrate the thick branches of the trees.

He could even hear the leaves whisking and flicking together, and when a man can discern this, he can hear the cushions of a mountain lion on a trail at night. Of course Dan Failing had never heard a mountain lion. Except on the railroad tracks between he had never really been away from cities in his life.

At once his thought went back to the doctor's words. Dan had a very retentive memory, as well as an extra fine imagination. The two always seem to go together. The words were still repeating themselves over and over in his ears, and the doctor's face was still before his eyes. It had been a kind face; the lips had even curled in a little smile of encouragement. But the doctor had been perfectly frank, entirely straightforward. Dan was glad that he had. At least, he was rid of the dreadful uncertainty. There had been no evasion in his verdict.

"I've made every test," he said. "They're pretty well shot. Of course, you can go to some sanitarium, if you've got the money. If you haven't--enjoy yourself all you can for about six months."

Dan's voice had been perfectly cool and sure when he replied. He had smiled a little, too. He was still rather proud of that smile. "Six months? Isn't that rather short?"

"Maybe a whole lot shorter. I think that's the limit."

There was the situation: Dan Failing had but six months to live. Of course, the doctor said, if he had the money he could go to a sanitarium. But he had spoken entirely hopelessly. Besides, Dan didn't have the money. He pushed all thought of sanitariums out of his mind. Instead, he began to wonder whether his mother had been entirely wise in her effort to keep him from the "rough games" of the boys of his own age. He realized now that he had been an under-weight all his life,--that the frailty that had thrust him to the edge of the grave had begun in his earliest boyhood. But it wasn't that he was born with physical handicaps. He had weighed a full ten pounds; and the doctor had told his father that a sturdier little chap was not to be found in any maternity bed in the whole city. But his mother was convinced that the child was delicate and must be sheltered. Never in all the history of his family, so far as Dan knew, had there been a death from the malady that afflicted him. Yet his sentence was signed and sealed.

But he harbored no resentment against his mother. It was all in the game. She had done what she thought was best. And he began to wonder in what way he could get the greatest pleasure from his last six months of life.

"Good Lord!" he suddenly breathed. "I may not even be here to see the snows come!" Perhaps there was a grim note in his voice. There was certainly no tragedy, no offensive sentimentality. He was looking the matter in the face. But it was true that Dan had always been partial to the winter season. When the snow lay all over the farmlands and bowed down the limbs of the trees, it had always wakened a curious flood of feelings in the wasted man. It seemed to him that he could remember other winters, wherein the snow lay for endless miles over an endless wilderness, and here and there were strange, many-toed tracks that could be followed in the icy dawns. He didn't ever know just what made the tracks, except that they were creatures of fang and talon that no law had ever tamed. But of course it was just a fancy. He wasn't in the least misled about it. He knew that he had never, in his lifetime, seen the wilderness. Of course his grandfather had been a frontiersman of the first order, and all his ancestors before him--a rangy, hardy breed whose wings would crumple in civilization--but he himself had always lived in cities. Yet the falling snows, soft and gentle but with a kind of remorselessness he could sense but could not understand, had always stirred him. He'd often imagined that he would like to see the forests in winter. He knew something about forests. He had gone one year to college and had studied all the forestry that the university heads would let him take. Later he had read endless books on the same subject. But the knowledge had never done him any good. Except for a few boyish dreams, he never imagined that it would.

In him you could see a reflection of the boy that played beside the pond of snow water, twenty years before. His dark gray eyes were still rather large and perhaps the wasted flesh around them made them seem larger than they were. But it was a little hard to see them, as he wore large glasses. His mother had been sure, years before, that he needed glasses; and she had easily found an oculist that agreed with her.

Now that he was alone on the path, the utter absence of color in his cheeks was startling. That meant the absence of red,--that warm glow of the blood, eager and alive in his veins. There was, indeed, another color, visible only because of the stark whiteness of his skin. He was newly shaven, and his lips and chin looked somewhat blue from the heavy growth of hair under the skin. Perhaps an observer would have noticed lean hands, with big-knuckled fingers, a rather firm mouth, and closely cropped dark hair. He was twenty-nine years of age, but he looked somewhat older. He knew now that he was never going to be any older. A doctor as sure of himself as the one he had just consulted couldn't possibly be mistaken.

It was rather refreshing to get into the park. Dan could think ever so much more clearly. He never could think in a crowd. Someway, the hurrying people always seemed to bewilder him. Here the leaves were flicking and rustling over his head, and the shadows made a curious patchwork on the green lawns. He became quite calm and reflective. And then he sat down on a park bench, just beneath the spreading limb of a great tree. He would sit here, he thought, until he finally decided what he would do with his remaining six months.

He hadn't been able to go to war. The recruiting officer had been very kind but most determined. The boys had brought him great tales of France. It might be nice to go to France and live in some country inn until he died. But he didn't have very long to think upon this vein. For at that instant the squirrel came down to see if he had a nut.

It was the squirrel of Destiny. But Dan didn't know it then.

Now it is true that it takes more than one generation for any wild creature to get completely away from its natural timidity. Quite often a person is met who has taken quail eggs from a nest and hatched them beneath the warm body of a domestic hen. Just what is the value of such a proceeding is rather hard to explain, as quail have neither the instincts nor the training to enjoy life in a barnyard. Yet occasionally it is done, and the little quail spend most of their days running frantically up and down the coop, yearning for the wild, free spaces for which they were created. But they haven't, as a rule, many days to spend in this manner. Mostly they rim until they die.

The rule is said to work both ways. A tame canary, freed, will usually try to return to his cage. And this is known to be true of human beings just as of the wild creatures. There are certain breeds of men, used to the far-lying hills, who, if inclosed in cities, run up and down them until they die. The Indians, for instance, haven't ever been able to adjust themselves to civilization. There are several thousand of them now where once were millions.

Bushy-tail was not particularly afraid of the human beings that passed up and down the park, because he had learned by experience that they usually attempted no harm to him. But, nevertheless, he had his instincts. He didn't entirely trust them. Occasionally a child would come with a bag of nuts, and he would sit on the grass not a dozen feet away to gather such as were thrown to him. But all the time he kept one sharp eye open for any sudden or dangerous motions. And every instinct warned him against coming nearer than a dozen feet. After several generations, probably the squirrels of this park would climb all over its visitors and sniff in their ears and investigate the back of their necks. But this wasn't the way of Bushy-tail. He had come too recently from the wild places. And he wondered, most intensely, whether this tall, forked creature had a pocket full of nuts. He swung down on the grass to see.

"Why, you little devil!" Dan said in a whisper. His eyes suddenly sparkled with de-light. And he forgot all about the doctor's words and his own prospects in his bitter regrets that he had not brought a pocketful of nuts. Unfortunately, he had never acquired the peanut habit. His mother had always thought it vulgar.

And then Dan did a curious thing. Even later, he didn't know why he did it, or what gave him the idea that he could decoy the squirrel up to him by doing it. That was his only purpose,--just to see how close the squirrel would come to him. He thought he would like to look into the bright eyes at close range. All he did was suddenly to freeze into one position,--in an instant rendered as motionless as the rather questionable-looking stone stork that was perched on the fountain.

He didn't know it, at the time, but it was a most meritorious piece of work. The truth was that he was acting solely by instinct. Men who have lived long in the wilderness learn a very important secret in dealing with wild animals. They know, in the first place, that intimacy with them is solely a matter of sitting still and making no sudden motions. It is motion, not shape, that frightens them. If a hunter is among a herd of deer and wishes to pick the bucks off, one by one, he simply sits still, moving his rifle with infinite caution, and the animal intelligence does not extend far enough to interpret him as an enemy. Instead of being afraid, the deer are usually only curious.

Dan simply sat still. The squirrel was very close to him, and Dan seemed to know by instinct that the movement of a single muscle would give him away. So he sat as if he were posing before a photographer's camera. The fact that he was able to do it is in itself important. It is considerably easier to exercise with dumb-bells for five minutes than to sit absolutely without motion for the same length of time. Hunters and naturalists acquire the art with training. It was therefore rather curious that Dan succeeded so well the first time he tried it. He had sense enough to relax first, before he froze. Thus he didn't put such a severe strain on his muscles. And this was another bit of wisdom that in a tenderfoot would have caused much wonder in certain hairy old hunters in the West.

The squirrel, after ten seconds had elapsed, stood on his haunches to see better. First he looked a long tune with his left eye. Then he turned his head and looked very carefully with his right. Then he backed off a short distance and tried to get a focus with both. Then he came some half-dozen steps nearer.

A moment before he had been certain that a living creature--in fact one of the most terrible and powerful living creatures in the world--had been sitting on. the park bench. Now his poor little brain was completely addled. He was entirely ready to believe that his eyes had deceived him.

All the time, Dan was sitting in perfectly plain sight. It wasn't as if he were hiding.

But the squirrel had learned to judge all life by its motion alone, and he was completely at a loss to interpret or understand a motionless figure.

Bushy-tail drew off a little further, fully convinced at last that his hopes of a nut from a child's hand were blasted. But he turned to look once more. The figure still sat utterly inert. And all at once he forgot his devouring hunger in the face of an overwhelming curiosity.

He came somewhat nearer and looked a long time. Then he made a half-circle about the bench, turning his. head as he moved. He was more puzzled than ever, but he was no longer afraid. His curiosity had become so intense that no room for fear was left. And then he sprang upon the park bench.

Dan moved then. The movement consisted of a sudden heightening of the light in his eyes. But the squirrel didn't see it. It takes a muscular response to be visible to the eyes of the wild things.

The squirrel crept slowly along the bench, stopping to sniff, stopping to stare with one eye and another, just devoured from head to tail with curiosity. And then he leaped on Dan's knee.

He was quite convinced, by now, that this warm perch on which he stood was the most singular and interesting object of his young life. It was true that he was faintly worried by the smell that reached his nostrils. But all it really did was further to incite his curiosity. He followed the leg up to the hip and then perched on the elbow. And an instant more he was poking a cold nose into Dan's neck.

But if the squirrel was excited by all these developments, its amazement was nothing compared to Dan's. It had been the most astounding incident in the man's life. He sat still, tingling with delight. And in a single flash of inspiration he knew he had come among his own people at last.

The creatures of the wild,--they were the folk he had always secretly loved and instinctively understood. His ancestors, for literally generations, had been frontiersmen and outdoor naturalists who never wrote books. Was it possible that they had bequeathed to him an understanding and love of the wild that most men did not have? But before he had time to meditate on this question, an idea seemed to pop and flame like a Roman candle in his brain. He knew where he would spend his last six months of life.

His own grandfather had been a hunter and trapper and frontiersman in a certain vast but little known Oregon forest. His son had moved to the Eastern cities, but in Dan's garret there used to be old mementoes and curios from these savage days,--a few claws and teeth, and a fragment of an old diary. The call had come to him at last. Tenderfoot though he was, Dan would go back to those forests, to spend his last six months of life among the wild creatures that made them their home.

II

The dinner hour found Dan Failing in the public library of Gitcheapolis, asking the girl who sat behind the desk if he might look at maps of Oregon. He got out the whole question without coughing once, but in spite of it she felt that he ought to be asking for California or Arizona maps, rather than Oregon. People did not usually go to Oregon to rid themselves of his malady. A librarian, as a rule, is a wonderfully well-informed person; but her mental picture of Oregon was simply one large rainstorm. She remembered that she used to believe that Oregon people actually grew webs between their toes, and the place was thus known as the Webfoot State. She didn't know that Oregon has almost as many climates as the whole of nature has in stock,-- snow in the east, rain in the north, winds in the west, and sunshine in the south, with all the grades between. There are certain sections where in midwinter all hunters who do not particularly care to sink over their heads in the level snow walk exclusively on snowshoes. There are others, not one hundred miles distant, where any kind of snowstorm is as rare a phenomenon as the seventeen-year locusts. Distances are rather vasty in the West. For instance, the map that Dan Failing looked at did not seem much larger than the map, say, of Maryland. Figures showed, however, that at least two counties of Oregon were each as large as the whole area of the former State.

He remembered that his grandfather had lived in Southern Oregon. He looked along the bottom of his map and discovered a whole empire, ranging from gigantic sage plains to the east to dense forests along the Pacific Ocean. Those sage flats, by the way, contain not only sage hens as thick as poultry in a henyard and jack rabbits of a particularly long-legged and hardy breed, but also America's one species of antelope. Had Dan known that this was true, had he only been aware that these antelope are without exception the fastest-running creatures upon the face of the earth, he might have been tempted to go there instead of to the land of his fathers. But all he saw on the map was a large brown space marked at exceedingly long intervals with the name of a fort or town. He began to search for Linkville.

Time was when Linkville was one of the principal towns of Oregon. Dan remembered the place because some of the time-yellowed letters his grandfather had sent him had been mailed at a town that bore this name. But he couldn't find Linkville on the map. Later he was to know the reason,--that the town, halfway between the sage plains and the mountains, had prospered and changed its name. He remembered that it was located on one of those great fresh-water lakes of Southern Oregon; so, giving up that search, he began to look for lakes. He found them in plenty,--vast, unmeasured lakes that seemed to be distributed without reason or sense over the whole southern end of the State. Near the Klamath Lakes, seemingly the most imposing of all the freshwater lakes that the map revealed, he found a city named Klamath Falls. He put the name down in his notebook.

The map showed a particularly high, farspreading range of mountains due west of the city. Of course they were the Cascades; the map said so very plainly. Then Dan knew he was getting home. His grandfather had lived and trapped and died in these same wooded hills. Finally he located and recorded the name of the largest city on the main railroad line that was adjacent to the Cascades.

The preparation for his departure took many days. He read many hooks on flora and fauna. He bought sporting equipment. Knowing the usual ratio between the respective pleasures of anticipation and realization, he did not hurry himself at all. And one midnight he boarded a west-bound train.

There were none that he cared about bidding good-by. The sudden realization of the fact brought a moment's wonder. He had not realized that he had led such a lonely existence. There were men who were fitted for living in cities, but perhaps he was not one of them. He saw the station lights grow dim as the train pulled out. Soon he could discern just a spark, here and there, from the city's outlying homes. And not long after this, the silence and darkness of the farm lands closed down upon the train.

He sat for a long time in the vestibule of the sleeping car, thinking in anticipation of this final adventure of his life. It is true that he had not experienced many adventures. He had lived most of them in imagination alone; or else, with tired eyeSj he had read of the exploits of other men. He was rather tremulous and exultant as he sank down into his berth.

He saw to it that at least a measure of preparation was made for his coming. That night a long wire went out to the Chamber of Commerce of one of the larger Southern Oregon cities. In it, he told the date of his arrival and asked certain directions. He wanted to know the name of some mountain rancher where possibly he might find board and room for the remainder of the summer and the fall. He wanted shooting, and he particularly cared to be near a river where trout might be found. They never came up Gitcheapolis River, or leaped for flies in the pond back of the courthouse. The further back from the paths of men, he wrote, the greater would be his pleasure. And he signed the wire with his full name: Dan Failing with a Henry in the middle, and a "III" at the end.

He usually didn't sign his name in quite this manner. The people of Gitcheapolis did not have particularly vivid memories of Dan's grandfather. But it might be that a legend of the gray, straight frontiersman who was his ancestor had still survived in these remote Oregon wilds. The use of the full name would do no harm.

Instead of hurting, it was a positive inspiration. The Chamber of Commerce of the busy little Oregon city was not usually exceptionally interested in stray hunters that wanted a boarding place for the summer. Its business was finding country homes for orchardists in the pleasant river valleys. But it happened that the recipient of the wire was one of the oldest residents, a frontiersman himself, and it was one of the traditions of the Old West that friendships were not soon forgotten. Dan Failing I had been a legend in the old trapping and shooting days when this man was young. So it came about that when Dan's train stopped at Cheyenne, he found a telegram waiting him:

"Any relation to Dan Failing of the Umpquaw Divide?"

Dan had never heard of the Umpquaw Divide, but he couldn't doubt but that the sender of the wire referred to his grandfather. He wired in the affirmative. The head of the Chamber of Commerce received the wire, read it, thrust it into his desk, and in the face of a really important piece of business proceeded to forget all about it. Thus it came about that, except for one thing, Dan Failing would have probably stepped off the train at his destination wholly unheralded and unmet. The one thing that changed his destiny was that at a meeting of a certain widely known fraternal order the next night, the Chamber of Commerce crossed trails with the Frontier in the person of another old resident who had his home in the farthest reaches of the Umpquaw Divide. The latter asked the former to come up for a few days' shooting--the deer being fatter and more numerous than any previous season since the days of the grizzlies. For it is true that one of the most magnificent breed of bears that ever walked the face of the earth once left their footprints, as of flour-sacks in the mud, from one end of the region to another.

"Too busy, I'm afraid," the Chamber of Commerce had replied. "But Lennox-- that reminds me. Do you remember old Dan Failing?

Lennox probed back into the years for a single instant, straightened out all the kinks of his memory in less time than the wind straightens out the folds of a flag, and turned a most interested face. "Remember him!" he exclaimed. "I should say I do." The middle-aged man half-closed his piercing, gray eyes. Those piercing eyes are a characteristic peculiar to the mountain men, and whether they come from gazing over endless miles of winter snow, or from some quality of steel that life in the mountains imbues, no one is quite able to determine.

"Listen, Steele," he said. "I saw Dan Failing make a bet once. I was just a kid, but I wake up in my sleep to marvel at it. We had a full long glimpse of a black-tail bounding up a long slope. It was just a spike-buck, and Dan Failing said he could take the left-hand spike off with one shot from his old Sharpens. Three of us bet hun--the whole thing in less than two seconds. With the next shot, he'd get the deer. He won the bet, and now if I ever forget Dan Failing, I want to die."

"You're just the man I'm looking for, then. You're not going out till the day after to-morrow?"

"No."

"On the limited, hitting here to-morrow morning, there's a grandson of Dan Failing. His name is Dan Failing too, and he wants to go up to your place to him. Stay all summer and pay board."

Lennox's eyes said that he couldn't believe it was true. After a while his tongue spoke, too. "Good Lord," he said. "I used to foller Dan around--like old Shag, before he died, followed Snowbird. Of course he can come. But he can't pay board."

It was rather characteristic of the mountain men,--that the grandson of Dan Failing couldn't possibly pay board. . But Steele knew the ways of cities and of men, and he only smiled. "He won't come, then," he explained.

"Anyway, have that out with him at the end of his stay. He wants fishing, and you've got that in the North fork. He wants shooting, and if there is a place in the United States with more wild animals around the back door than at your house, I don't know where it is. Moreover, you're a thousand miles back--"

"Only one hundred, if you must know. But Steele--do you suppose he's the man his grandfather was before him--that all the Failings have been since the first days of the Oregon trail? If he is--well, my hat's off to him before he steps off the train."

The mountaineer's bronzed face was earnest and intent in the bright lights of the club. Steele thought he had known this breed. Now he began to have doubts of his own knowledge. "He won't be; don't count on it," he said humbly. "The Failings have done much for this region, and I'm glad enough to do a little to pay it back, but don't count much on this Eastern boy. He's lived in cities; besides, he's a sick man. He said so in his wire. You ought to know it before you take him in."

The bronzed face changed; possibly a shadow of disappointment came into his eyes. "A lunger, eh?" Lennox repeated. "Yes--it's true that if he'd been like the other Failings, he'd never have been that. Why, Steele, you couldn't have given that old man a cold if you'd tied him in the Rogue River overnight. Of course you couldn't count on the line keeping up forever. But I'll take him, for the memory of his grandfather."

"You're not afraid to?"

"Afraid, Hell! He can't infect those two strapping children of mine. Snowbird weighs one hundred and twenty pounds and is hard as steel. Never knew a sick day in her life. And you know Bill, of course."

Yes, Steele knew Bill. Bill weighed two hundred pounds, and he would choose the biggest of the steers he drove down to the lower levels in the winter and, twisting its horns, would make it lay over on its side. Besides, both of the men assumed that Dan must be only in the first stages of his malady.

And even as the men talked, the train that bore Dan Failing to the home of his ancestors was entering for the first time the dark forests of pine and fir that make the eternal background of the Northwest. The wind came cool and infinitely fresh into the windows of the sleeping car, and it brought, as camels bring myrrh from the East, strange, pungent odors of balsam and mountain flower and warm earth, cooling after a day of blasting sun. And these smells all came straight home to

Dan. He was wholly unable to understand the strange feeling of familiarity that he had with them, a sensation that in his dreams he had known them always, and that he must never go out of the range of them again.

III

Dan didn't see his host at first. For the first instant he was entirely engrossed by a surging sense of disappointment,--a feeling that he had been tricked and had only come to another city after alL He got down on to the gravel of the station yard, and out on the gray street pavement he heard the clang of a trolley car. Trolley cars didn't fit into his picture of the West at all. Many automobiles were parked just beside the station, some of them foreign cars of expensive makes, such as he supposed would be wholly unknown on the frontier. A man in golf clothes brushed his shoulder.

It wasn't a large city; but there was certainly lack of any suggestion of the frontier. But there were a number of things that Dan Failing did not know about the West. One of the most important of them was the curious way in which wildernesses and busy cities are sometimes mixed up indiscriminately together, and how one can step out of a modem country club to hear the coyotes wailing on the hills. He really had no right to feel disappointed. He had simply come to the real West--that bewildering land in which To-morrow and Yesterday sit right next to each other, with no Today between. The cities, often built on the dreams of the future, sometimes are modem to such a point that they give many a sophisticated Eastern man a decided shock. But quite often this quality extends to the corporation limits and not a step further. Then, likely as not, they drop sheer off, as over a precipice, into the utter wildness of the Past.

Dan looked up to the hills, and he felt better. He couldn't see them plainly. The faint smoke of a distant forest fire half obscured them. Yet he saw fold on fold of ridges of a rather peculiar blue in color, and even his untrained eyes could see that they were clothed in forests of evergreen. It is a strange thing about evergreen forests that they never, even when one is close to them, appear to be really green. To a distant eye, they range all the way from lavender to a pale sort of blue for which no name has ever been invented. Just before dark, when, as all mountaineers know, the sky turns green, the forests are simply curious, dusky shadows. The pines are always dark. Perhaps, after all, they are simply the symbol of the wilderness,--eternal, silent, and in a vague way rather dark and sad. No one who really knows the mountains can completely get away from their tone of sadness. Over the heads of the green hills Dan could see a few great peaks; McLaughlin, even and regular as a painted mountain; Wagner, with queer white gashes where the snow still lay in its ravines, and to the southeast the misty range of snowcovered hills that were the Siskeyous. He felt decidedly better. And when he saw old Silas Lennox waiting patiently beside the station, he felt he had come to the right place.

It would be interesting to explain why Dan at once recognized the older man for the breed he was. But unfortunately, there are certain of the many voices that speak within the minds of human beings of which scientists have never been able to take phonographic records. They simply whisper their messages, and their hearer, without knowing why, knows that he has heard the truth. Silas Lennox was not dressed in a way that would distinguish him. It was true that he wore a flannel shirt, riding trousers, and rather heavy, leathern boots. But sportsmen all over the face of the earth wear this costume at sundry times. Mountain men have a peculiar stride by which experienced persons can occasionally recognize them; but Silas Lennox was standing still when Dan got his first glimpse of him. The case resolves itself into a simple matter of the things that could be read in Lennox's face.

Dan disbelieved wholly in a book that told how to read characters at sight.

Yet at the first glance of the lean, bronzed face his heart gave a curious little bound. A pair of gray eyes met his,--two fine black points in a rather hard gray iris. They didn't look past him, or at either side of him, or at his chin or his forehead. They looked right at his own eyes. The skin around the eyes was burned brown by the sun, and the flesh was so lean that the cheek bones showed plainly. The mouth was straight; but yet it was neither savage nor cruel. It was simply determined.

But the strangest part of all was that Dan felt an actual sense of familiarity with this kind of man. To his knowledge, he had never known one before; and it was extremely doubtful if, in his middle-western city, he had even seen the type. In spite of the fact that he thinks nothing of starting out thirty miles across the snow on snowshoes, the mountain man cannot be called an extensive traveler. He plans to go to some great city once in a lifetime and dreams about it of nights, but rather often the Death that is every one's nextdoor neighbor in the wilderness comes in and cheats him out of the trip. Few of the breed had ever come to Gitcheapolis. Yet all his life, Dan felt, he had known this straight, gray-eyed mountain breed even better than he knew the boys that went to college with him. At the time he didn't stop to wonder at the feeling. He was too busy looking about. But the time was to come when he would wonder and conclude that it was just another bit of evidence pointing to the same conclusion. And besides this unexplainable feeling of familiarity, he felt a sudden sense of peace, even a quiet sort of exultation, such as a man feels when he gets back into his own home country at last.

Lennox came up with a light, silent tread and extended his hand. "You're Dan Failing's grandson, aren't you?" he asked. "I'm Silas Lennox, who used to know him when he lived on the Divide. You are coming to spend the summer and fall on my ranch."

The immediate result of these words, besides relief, was to set Dan wondering how the old mountaineer had recognized him. He wondered if he had any physical resemblance to his grandfather. But this hope was shot to earth at once. His telegram had explained about his malady, and of course the mountaineer had picked him out simply because he had the mark of the disease on his face. As he shook hands, he tried his best to read the mountaineer's expression. It was all too plain: an undeniable look of disappointment.

The truth was that even in spite of all the Chamber of Commerce head had told him, Lennox had still hoped to find some image of the elder Dan Failing in the face and body of his grandson. But at first there seemed to be none at all. The great hunter and trapper who had tamed the wilderness about the region of the Divide--as far as mortal man could tame it--had a skin that was rather the color of old leather. The face of this young man was wholly without tinge of color. Because of the thick glasses, Lennox could not see the young man's eyes; but he didn't think it likely they were at all like the eyes with which the elder Failing saw his way through the wilderness at night. Of course he was tall, just as the famous frontiersman had been, but while the elder weighed one hundred and ninety pounds, bone and muscle, this man did not touch one hundred and thirty. Evidently the years had brought degeneracy to the Failing dan. Lennox was desolated by the thought.

He helped Dan with his bag to a little wiry automobile that waited beside the station. They got into the two front seats.

"You'll be wondering at my taking you in a car--clear to the Divide," Lennox explained. "But we mountain men can't afford to drive horses any more where a car will go. This time of year I can make it fairly easy--only about fifteen miles on low gear. But in the winter--it's either a case of coming down on snowshoes or staying there."

And a moment later they were starting up the long, curved road that led to the Divide.

During the hour that they were crossing over the foothills, on the way to the big timber, Silas Lennox talked a great deal about the frontiersman that had been Dan's grandfather. A mountain man does not use profuse adjectives. He talks very simply and very straight, and often there are long silences between his sentences. Yet he conveys his ideas with entire clearness.

Dan realized at once that if he could be, in Lennox's eyes, one fifth of the man his grandfather had been, he would never have to fear again, the look of disappointment with which his host had greeted him at the station. But instead of reaching that high place, he had only--death. He was never to be one of this strong breed from which his people sprang. Always they would accept him for the memories that they held of his ancestors, pity him for his weakness, and possibly be kind enough to deplore his death. He never need fear any actual expressions of scorn. Lennox had a natural refinement that forbade it. Dan never knew a more intense desire than that to make good in the eyes of these mountain men. Far back, they had been his own people; and all men know that the upholding of a family's name and honor has been one of the greatest impulses for good conduct and great deeds since the beginnings of civilization. But Dan pushed the hope out of his mind at once. He knew what his destiny was in these quiet hills. And it was true that he began to have secret regrets that he had come. But it wasn't that he was disappointed in the land that was opening up before him. It fulfilled every promise. His sole reason for regrets lay in the fact that now the whole mountain world would know of the decay that had come upon his people. Perhaps it would have been better to have left them to their traditions.

He had never dreamed that the fame of his grandfather had spread so far. For the first ten miles, Dan listened to stories,--legends of a cold nerve that simply could not be shaken; of a powerful, tireless physique; of moral and physical strength that was seemingly without limit. Then, as the foothills began to give way to the higher ridges, and the shadow of the deeper forests fell upon the narrow, brown road, there began to be long gaps in the talk. And soon they rode in utter silence, evidently both of them absorbed in their own thoughts.

Dan did not wonder at it at all. Perhaps he began to faintly understand the reason for the silence and the reticence that is such a predominant trait in the forest men. There is a quality in the big timber that doesn't make for conversation, and no one has ever been completely successful in explaining what it is. Perhaps there is a feeling of insignificance, a sensation that is particularly insistent in the winter snows. No man can feel like talking very loudly when he is the only living creature within endless miles. The trees, towering and old, seem to ignore him as a being too unimportant to notice. And besides, the silence of the forest itself seems to get into the spirit, and the great, quiet spaces that he between tree and tree simply dry up the springs of conversation. Dan did not feel oppressed at all. He merely seemed to fall into the spirit of the woods, and no words came to his lips. He began to watch the ever-changing vista that the curving road revealed.

First there had been brown hills, and here and there great heaps of stone. The brush had been rather scrubby, and the trees somewhat sickly and brown. But now, as the men mounted higher, they were coming into open forest. The trees stood one and one, perfect, dark-limbed, and only the carpet of their needles lay between. The change was evidenced in the streams, too. They seemingly had not suffered from the drought that had sucked up the valley streams. They were faster, whiter with foam, and the noise of their falling waters carried farther through the still woods. The road followed the long shoulder of a ridge, an easy grade of perhaps six per cent, but Dan counted ridges sloping off until he was tired.

By now the smaller wild things of the mountains began to present themselves a breathless instant beside the road. These little people have an actual purpose in the hills other than to furnish food for the larger forest creatures. They give a note of sociability, of companionship, that is sorely needed to dull the edge of the utter, stark lonesomeness and severity that is the usual tone of the mountains. The fact that they all live under the snow in winter is (me reason why this season is especially dreadful to the spirit.

Every tree trunk seemed to have its chipmunks, and they all appeared to be suffering from the same delusion. They all were afflicted with the idea that the car was trying to cut off their retreat, and only by crossing the road in front of it could they save themselves. This idea is a particularly prevalent one with wild animals; and it is the same instinct that makes a domestic cow almost invariably cross the road in front of a motorist. And it also explains why certain cowardly animals, such as the wolf or cougar, will sometimes seemingly without a cause on earth, make a desperate charge on a hunter. They think their retreat is cut off, and they have to fight. Again and again the chipmunks crossed at the risk of their lives. Sometimes the two men saw those big, flat-footed rabbits that are especially constructed for mowing about in the winter snows, and more than once the grouse rose with a whir and beat of wings.

Every mile was an added delight to Dan. Not even wine could have brought a brighter sparkle to his eyes. He had begun to experience a vague sort of excitement, an emotion that was almost kin to exultation, over the constant stir and movement of the forest life. He didn't know that a bird dog feels the same when it gets to the uplands where the quail are hiding. He had no acquaintance with bird dogs whatever. He hadn't remembered that he had qualities in common with them,--a long line of ancestors who had lived by hunting.

Once, as they stopped the car to refill the radiator from a mountain stream, Lennox looked at him with sudden curiosity. "You are getting a thrill out of this, aren't you?" he asked wonderingly.

It was a curious tone. Perhaps it was a hopeful tone, too. He spoke as if he hardly understood.

"A thrill!" Dan echoed. He spoke as a man speaks in the presence of some great wonder. "Good Heavens, I never saw anything like it in my life."

"In this very stream," the mountaineer told him joyously, "you may occasionally catch trout that weigh three pounds."

But as he got back into the car, the look of interest died out of Lennox's eyes. Of course any man would be somewhat excited by his first glimpse of the wilderness. It was not that he had inherited any of the traits of his grandfather. It was absurd to hope that he had. And he would soon get tired of the silences and want to go back to his cities. He told his thought--that it would all soon grow old to him; and Dan turned almost in anger.

"You don't know," he said. "I didn't know myself, how I would feel about it. I'm never going to leave the hills again."

"You don't mean that."

"But I do." He tried to speak further, but he coughed instead. "But I couldn't if I wanted to. That cough tells you why, I guess."

"You mean to say--" Silas Lennox turned in amazement. "You mean that you're a--a goner? That you've given up hope of recovering?

"That's the impression I meant to convey. I've got a little over four months-- though I don't see that I'm any weaker than I was when the doctor said I had six months. Those four will take me all through the fall and the early winter.

And I hope you won't feel that you've been imposed upon--to have a dying man on your hands."

"It isn't that." Silas Lennox threw his car into gear and started up the long grade. And he drove clear to the top of it and into another glen before he spoke again. Then he pointed to what looked to Dan like a brown streak that melted into the thick brush. "That was a deer," he said slowly. "Just a glimpse, but your grandfather could have got him between the eyes. Most like as not, though, he'd have let him go. He never killed except when he needed meat. But that--as you say--ain't the impression I'm trying to convey."

He seemed to be groping for words.

"What is it, Mr. Lennox?" Dan asked.

"Instead of being sorry, I'm mighty glad you've come," Lennox told him. "It's not that I expect you to be like your grandfather. You haven't had his chance. But it's always the way of true men, the world over, to come back to their own kind to die. That deer we just saw--he's your people, and so are all these ranchers that grub their lives out of the forests--they are your people too. The bears and the elk, and even the porcupines. Though you likely won't care for 'em, it's almost as if they were your grandfather's own folks. And you couldn't have pleased the old man's old friends any better, or done more for his memory, than to come back to his own land for your last days."

There were great depths of meaning in the simple words. There were significances, such as the love that the mountain men have for their own land, that came but dimly to Dan's perceptions. The words were strange, yet Dan intuitively understood. It was as if a prodigal son had returned at last, and although his birthright was squandered and he came only to die. the people of his home would give him kindness and forgiveness, even though they could not give him their respect.

IV

The Lennox home was a typical mountain ranch-house,--square, solid, comforting in storm and wind. Bill was out to the gate when the car drove up. He was a son of his father, a strong man in body and personality. He too had heard of the elder Failing, and he opened his eyes when he saw the slender youth that was his grandson. And he led the way into the white-walled living room.

The shadows of twilight were just falling; and Bill had already lighted a fire in the fireplace to remove the chill that always descends with the mountain night. The whole long room was ruddy and cheerful in its glare. At once the elder Lennox drew a chair close to it for Dan.

"You must be chilly and worn-out from the long ride," he suggested quietly. He spoke in the tone a strong man invariably uses toward an invalid. But while a moment before Dan had welcomed the sight of the leaping, life-giving flames, he felt a curious resentment at the words.

"I'm not cold," he said. "It's hardly dark yet. I'd sooner go outdoors and look around."

The elder man regarded him curiously, perhaps with the faintest glimmer of admiration. "You'd better wait till to-morrow, Dan," he replied. "Bill will have supper soon, anyway. To-morrow we'll walk up the ridge and I'll see if I can show you a deer. You don't want to overdo too much, right at first."

"But, good Heavens! I'm not going to try to spare myself while I'm here. It's too late for that."

"Of course--but sit down now, anyway. I'm sorry that Snowbird isn't here."

"Snowbird is--"

"My daughter. My boy, she can make a biscuit! That's not her name, of course, but we've always called her that. She got tired of keeping house and is working this summer. Poor Bill has to keep house for her, and no wonder he's eager to take the stock down to the lower levels. I only wish he hadn't brought 'em up this spring at all; I've lost dozens from the coyotes."

"But a coyote can't kill cattle--"

"It can if it has hydrophobia, a common thing in the varmints this time of year. But as I say. Bill will take the stock down next season. and then Snowbird's work will be through, and she'll come back here."

"Then she's down in the valley?"

"Far from it. She's a mountain girl if one ever lived. Perhaps you don't know the recent policy of the forest service to hire women when they can be obtained. It was a policy started in wartimes and kept up now because it is economical and efficient. She and a girl from college have a cabin not five miles from here on old Bald Mountain, and they're doing look-out duty."

Dan wondered intensely what lookout duty might be. His thoughts went back to his early study of forestry. "You see, Dan," Lennox said in explanation, "the government loses thousands of dollars every year by forest fire. A fire can be stopped easily if it is seen soon after it starts. But let it burn awhile, in this dry season, and it's a terror--a wall of flame that races through the forests and can hardly be stopped. And maybe you don't realize how enormous this region is--literally hundreds of miles across. We're the last outpost--there are four cabins, if you can find them, in the first seventy miles back to town. So they have to put lookouts on the high points, and now they're coming to the use of aeroplanes so they can keep even a better watch. All summer and until the rains come in the fall, they have to guard every minute, and even then sometimes the fires get away from them. And one of the first things a forester learns, Dan, is to be careful with fire."

"Is that the way they are started--from the carelessness of campers?"

"Partly. There's an old rule in the hills: put out every fire before you leave it. Be careful with the cigar butts, too--even the coals of a pipe. But of course the lightning starts many fires, and, I regret to say, hundreds of them are started with matches."

"But why on earth--"

"It doesn't make very good sense, does it? Well, one reason is that certain stockmen think that a burned forest makes good range--that the undervegetation that springs up when the trees are burned makes good feed for stock. And you must know, too, that there are two kinds of men in the mountains. One kind--the real mountain man, such as your grandfather was--lives just as well, just as clean as the ranchers in the valley. Some of this kind are trappers or herders. But there's another class too--the most unbelievably shiftless, ignorant people in America. They have a few acres to raise crops, and they kill deer for their hides, and most of all they make their living fighting forest fires. A fire means work for every hill-billy in the region--often five or six dollars a day and better food than they're used to. Moreover, they can loaf on the job, put in claims for extra hours, and make what to them is a fortune.

"You'll likely see a few of the breed before--before your visit here is ended. There's a family of 'em not three miles away--and that's real neighborly in the mountains--by the name of Cranston. Bert Cranston traps a little and makes moonshine; you'll probably see plenty of him before the trip is over. Sometime I'll tell you of a little difficulty that I had with him once. You needn't worry about him coming to this house; he's already received his instructions in that Batter.

"But I see I'm getting all tangled up in my traces. Snowbird and a girl friend from college got jobs this summer as lookouts--all through the forest service they are hiring women for the work. They are more vigilant than men, less inclined to take chances, and work cheaper. These two girls have a cabin near a spring, and they cook their own food, are making what is big wages in the morn-I'm rather hoping she'll drop over for few minutes to-night."

"Good Lord--does she travel over these hills in the darkness?"

The mountaineer laughed--a delighted sound that came somewhat curiously from the bearded lips of the stern, dark man. "Dan, I'll swear she's afraid of nothing that walks the face of the earth--and it isn't because she hasn't had experiences either. She's a dead shot with a pistol, for one thing. She's physically strong, and every muscle is hard as nails. She used to have Shag, too--the best dog in all these mountains. She's a mountain girl, I tell you; whoever wins her has got to be able to tame her!" The mountaineer laughed again. "I sent her to school, of course, but there was only one boy she'd look at--the athletic coach I And it wasn't his fault that he didn't follow her back to the mountains."

The call to supper came then, and Dan got his first sight of mountain food. There were potatoes, newly dug, mountain vegetables that were crisp and cold, a steak of peculiar shape, and a great bowl of purple berries to be eaten with sugar and cream. Dan's appetite was not as a rule particularly good. But evidently the long ride had affected him. He simply didn't have the moral courage to refuse when the elder Lennox heaped his plate.

"Good Heavens, I can't eat all that," he said, as it was passed to him. But the others laughed and told him to take heart.

He took heart. It was a singular thing, but at that first bite his sudden confidence in his gustatory ability almost overwhelmed him. All his life he had avoided meat. His mother had always been convinced that such a delicate child as he had been could not properly digest it. But all at once he decided to forego his mother's philosophies for good and all. There was certainly nothing to be gained by following them any longer. So he cut himself a bite of the tender steak--fully half as generous as the bites that Bill was consuming across the table. And its first flavor simply filled him with delight.

"What is this meat?" he asked. "I've certainly tasted it before."

"I'll bet a few dollars that you haven't, If you've lived all your life in the Middle West," Lennox answered. "Maybe you've got what the scientists call an inherited memory of it. It's the kind of meat your grandfather used to live on--venison."

Both of them had seemed pleased that he liked the venison. And both seemed boyishly eager to test his reaction to the great, wild huckleberries that were the dessert of the simple meal. He tried them with much ceremony.

Their flavor really surprised him. They had a tang, a fragrance that was quite unlike anything he had ever tasted, yet which brought a curious flood of dim, half-understood memories. It seemed to him that always he had stood on the hillsides, picking these berries as they grew, and staining his lips with them. But at once he pushed the thoughts out of his mind, thinking that his imagination was playing tricks upon him. And soon after this, Lennox led him out of the house for his first glimpse of the hills in the darkness.

They walked together out to the gate, across the first of the wide pastures where, at certain seasons, Lennox kept his cattle; and at last they came out upon the tree-covered ridge. The moon was just rising. They could see it casting a curious glint over the very tips of the pines. But it couldn't get down between them. They stood too close, too tall and thick for that. And for a moment, Dan's only sensation was one of silence.

"You have to stand still a moment, to really know anything," Lennox told him.

They. both stood still. Dan was as motionless as that day in the park, long weeks before, when the squirrel had climbed on his shoulder. The first effect was a sensation that the silence was deepening around them. It wasn't really true. It was simply that he had become aware of the little continuous sounds of which usually he was unconscious, and they tended to accentuate the hush of the night. He heard his watch ticking in his pocket, the whispered stir of his own breathing, and he was quite certain that he could hear the fevered beat of his own heart in his breast. But then slowly he began to become aware of other sounds, so faint and indistinct that he really could not be sure that he heard them. There was a faint rustle and stir, as of the tops of the pine trees far away. Possibly he heard the wind too, the faintest whisper in the world through the underbrush. And finally, most wonderful of all, he began to hear one by one, over the ridge on which he stood, little whispered sounds of living creatures stirring in the thickets. He knew, just as all mountaineers know, that the wilderness about him was stirring and pulsing with life. Some of the sounds were quite clear--an occasional stir of a pebble or the crack of a twig, and some, like the faintest twitching of leaves in the brush not ten feet distant, could only be guessed at.

"What is making the sounds?" he asked.

He didn't know it, at the time, but Lennox turned quickly toward him. It wasn't that the question had surprised the mountaineer.

Rather it was the tone in which Dan had spoken. It was perfectly cool, perfectly selfcontained.

"The one right close is a chipmnnk. I don't know what the others are; no one ever does know. Perhaps ground squirrels, or rabbits, or birds, and maybe even one of those harmless old black bears who is curious about the house. The bears have more curiosity than they can well carry around, and they say they'll sometimes come up and put their front feet on a window sill of a house, and peer through the window. They must think men are the craziest things! And of course it might be a coyote--and a mad one at that. I guess I told you that they're subject to rabies at this time of year. I'll confess I'd rather have it be anything else. And tell me--can you smell anything--"

"Good Lord, Lennox I I can smell all kinds of things."

"I'm glad. Some men can't. No one can enjoy the woods if he can't smell. Part of the smells are of flowers, and part of balsam, and God only knows what the others are. They are just the wildemess--"

Dan could not only perceive the smells and sounds, but he felt that they were leaving an imprint on the very fiber of his soul. He knew one thing. He knew he could never forget this first introduction to the mountain night. The whole scene moved him in strange, deep ways in which he had never been stirred before; it left him exultant and, in deep wells of his nature far below the usual cm-rents of excitement, a little excited too. And all the time he had that indefinable sense of familiarity, a knowledge that this was his own land, and after a long, long time of wandering in far places, he had come back to it.

Then both of them were startled out of their reflections by the clear, unmistakable sound of footsteps on the ridge. Both of them turned, and Lennox laughed softly in the darkness. "My daughter," he said. "I knew she wouldn't be afraid to come."

Dan could see only Snowbird's outline at first, just her shadow against the moonlit hillside. His glasses were none too good at long range. And possibly, when she came within range, the first thing that he noticed about her was her stride. The girls he knew didn't walk in quite that free, strong way. She took almost a man-size step; and yet it was curious that she did not seem ungraceful. Dan had a distinct impression that she was floating down to him on the moonlight. She seemed to come with such unutterable smoothness. And then he heard her call lightly through the darkness.

The sound gave him a distinct sense of surprise. Some way, he hadn't associated a voice like this with a mountain girl; he had supposed that there would be so many harshening influences in this wild place. Yet the tone was as clear and full as a trained singer's. It was not a high voice; and yet it seemed simply brimming, as a cup brims with wine, with the rapture of life. It was a self-confident voice too, wholly unaffected and sincere, and wholly without embarrassment.

Then she came close, and Dan saw the moonlight on her face. . And so it came about, whether in dreams or wakefulness, he could see nothing else for many hours to come.

Beauty, after all, is wholly a matter of the nearest possible approach to the physical perfection that many centuries of human faces have established as a standard. Thus perfection in this case does not mean some ideal that has been imaged by a poet, but just the nearest approach to the perfect physical body that nature intended, and which is the flawless example of the type that composes the race. Thus a typical feature is the most beautiful, and by this reasoning a composite picture of all the young girl faces in the Anglo-Saxon nations would be the most beautiful face that any painter could conceive. It follows that health is above all the most essential quality to beauty, because disease, from the nature of things, means thwarted growth that could not possibly reach the typical of the race.

The girl who stood in the moonlight had health. She was simply vibrant with health. It brought a light to her eyes, and a color to her cheeks, and life and shimmer to her moonlit hair. It brought curves to her body, and strength and firmness to her limbs, and the grace of a deer to her carriage. Whether she had regular features or not Dan would have been unable to state. He didn't even notice. They weren't important when health was present. Yet there was nothing of the coarse or bold or voluptuous about her. She was just a slender girl, perhaps twenty years of age, and weighing even less than the figure occasionally to be read in the health magazines for girls of her height. And she was fresh and cool beyond all words to tell.

And Dan had no delusions about her attitude toward him. For a long instant she turned her keen, young eyes to his white, thin face; and at once it became abundantly evident that beyond a few girlish speculations she felt no interest in him. After a single moment of rather strained, polite conversation with Dan--just enough to satisfy her idea of the conventions--she began a thrilling girlhood tale to her father. And she was still telling it when they reached the house.

Dan held a chair for her in front of the fireplace, and she took it with entire naturalness. He was careful to put it where the firelight was at its height. He wanted to see its effect on the flushed cheeks, the soft dark hair. And then, standing in the shadows, he simply watched her. With the eye of an artist he delighted in her gestures, her rippling enthusiasm, her utter, irrepressible girlishness that all of Time had not years enough to kill.

He decided that she had gray eyes. Gray eyes seemed to be characteristic of the mountain people. Sometimes, when the shadows fell across them, they looked very dark, as if the pines had been reflected in them all day and the image had not yet faded out. But in an instant the shadow flicked away and left only light,--light that danced and light that laughed and light that went into him and did all manner of things to his spirit.

Bill stood watching her, his hands deep in his pockets, evidently a companion of the best. Her father gazed at her with amused tolerance. And Dan,--he didn't know in just what way he did look at her. And he didn't have time to decide. In less than fifteen minutes, and wholly without warning, she sprang up from her chair and started toward the door.

"Good Lord!" Dan breathed. "If you make such sudden motions as that I'll have heart failure. Where are you going now?"

"Back to my watch," she answered, her tone wholly lacking the personal note which men have learned to expect in the voices of women.

And an instant later the three of them saw her retreating shadow as she vanished among the pines.

Dan had to be helped to bed. The long ride had been too hard on his shattered lungs; and nerves and body collapsed an instant after the door was closed behind the departing girl. He laughed weakly and begged their pardon; and the two men were really very gentle. They told him it was their own fault for permitting him to overdo. Lennox himself blew out the candle in the big, cold bedroom.

Dan saw the door close behind him, and he had an instant's glimpse of the long sweep of moonlit ridge that stretched beneath the window. Then, all at once, seemingly without warning, it simply blinked out. Not until the next morning did he really know why. Insomnia was an old acquaintance of Dan's, and he had expected to have some trouble in getting to sleep. His only real trouble was waking up again when Lennox called him to breakfast. He couldn't believe that the light at his window shade was really that of morning.

"Good Heavens!" his host exploded. "You sleep the sleep of the just."

Dan was about to tell him that on the contrary he was a very nervous sleeper, but he thought better of it. Something had surely happened to his insomnia. The next instant he even forgot to wonder about it in the realization that his tired body had been wonderfully refreshed. He had no dread now of the long tramp up the ridge that his host had planned.

But first came target practice. In Dan's baggage he had a certain very plain but serviceable sporting rifle of about thirty-forty caliber,--a gun that the information department of the large sporting-goods store in Gitcheapolis had recommended for his purpose. Except for the few moments in the store, Dan had never held a rifle in his hands.

Of course the actual aiming of a rifle is an extremely simple proposition. A man with fair use of his hands and eyes can pick it up in less time than it takes to tell it. The fine art of marksmanship consists partly in the finer sighting,-- the instinctive realization of just what fraction of the front sight should be visible through the rear. But most of all it depends on the control that the nerves have over the muscles. Some men are born rifle shots; and on others it is quite impossible to thrust any skill whatever.

The nerve impulses and the muscular reflexes must be exquisitely tuned, so that the finger presses back on the trigger the identical instant that the mark is seen on the line of the sights. One quarter of a second's delay will usually disturb the aim. There must be no muscular jerk as the trigger is pressed. Shooting was never a sport for blasted nerves. And usually such attributes as the ability to judge distances, the speed and direction of a fleeing object, and the velocity of the wind can only be learned by tireless practice.

When Dan first took the rifle in his hands, Lennox was rather amazed at the ease and naturalness with which he held it. It seemed to come up naturally to his shoulder. Lennox scarcely had to tell him how to rest the butt and to drop his chin as he aimed. He began to look rather puzzled. Dan seemed to know all these things by instinct. The first shot, Dan hit the trunk of a five-foot pine at thirty paces.

"But I couldn't very well have missed it!" he replied to Lennox's cheer. "You see, I aimed at the middle--but I just grazed the edge."

The second shot was not so good, missing the tree altogether. And it was a singular thing that he aimed longer and tried harder on this shot than on the first. The third time he tried still harder, and made by far the worst shot of all.

"What's the matter?" he demanded. "I'm getting worse all the time."

Lennox didn't know for sure. But he made a long guess. "It might be beginner's luck," he said, "but I'm inclined to think you're trying too hard. Take it easier--depend more on your instincts. Some marksmen are born good shots and cook themselves trying to follow rules. It might be, by the longest chance, that you're one of them--at least it won't hurt to try."

Dan's reply was to lift the rifle lightly to his shoulder, glance quickly along the trigger, and fire. The bullet struck within one inch of the center of the pine.

For a long second Lennox gazed at him in open-mouthed astonishment. "My stars, boy!" he cried at last. "Was I mistaken in thinking you were a born tenderfoot--after all? Can it be that a little of your old grandfather's skill has been passed down to you? But you can't do it again."

But Dan did do it again. If anything, the bullet was a little nearer the center. And then he aimed at a more distant tree.

But the hammer snapped down ineffectively on the breech. He turned with a look of question.

"Your gun only holds five shots," Lennox explained. Reloading, Dan tried a more difficult target--a trunk almost one hundred yards distant. Of course it would have been only child's play to an experienced hunter; but to a tenderfoot it was the difficult mark indeed. Twice out of four shots Dan hit the tree trunk, and one of his two hits was practically a bull's-eye. His two misses were the result of the same mistake he had made before,--attempting to hold his aim too long.

The shots rang far through the quiet woods, long-drawn from the echoes that came rocking back from the hills. In contrast with the deep silence that is really an eternal part of the mountains, the sound seemed preternaturally loud. All over the great sweep of canyon, the wild creatures heard and were startled. One could easily imagine the Columbian deer, gone to their buckbrush to sleep, springing up and lifting pointed ears. There is no more graceful action in the whole animal world than this first, startled spring of a frightened buck. Then old Woof, feeding in the berry bushes, heard the sound too. Woof has considerably more understanding than most of the wild inhabitants of the forest, and maybe that is why he left his banquet and started falling all over his awkward self in descending the hill. It might be that Lennox would want to procure his guest a sample of bear steak; and Woof didn't care to be around to suggest such a thing. At least, that would be his train of thought according to those naturalists who insist on ascribing human intelligence to all the forest creatures. But it is true that Woof had learned to recognize a rifle shot, and he feared it worse than anything on earth.

Far away on the ridge top, a pair of wolves sat together with no more evidence of life than two shadows. One of the most effective accomplishments a wolf possesses is its ability to freeze into a motionless thing, so the sharpest eye can scarcely detect him in the thickets. It is an advantage in hunting, and it is an even greater advantage when being hunted. Yet at the same second they sprang up, simply seemed to spin in the dead pine needles, and brought up with sharp noses pointed and ears erect, facing the valley.

A human being likely would have wondered at their action. It is doubtful that human ears could have detected that faint tremor in the air which was all that was left of the rifle report. But of course this is a question that would be extremely difficult to prove; for as a rule the senses of the larger forest creatures, with the great exception of scent, are not as perfectly developed as those of a human being. A wolf can see better than a man in the darkness, but not nearly as far in the daylight. But the wolves knew this sound. Too many times they had seen their pack-fellows die in the snow when such a report as this, only intensified a thousand times, cracked at them through the winter air. No animal in all the forest has been as relentlessly hunted as the wolves, and they have learned their lessons. For longer years than most men would care to attempt to count, men have waged a ceaseless war upon them. And they have learned that their safety lies in flight.

Very quietly, and quite without panic, the wolves turned and headed farther into the forests. Possibly no other animal would have been frightened at such a distance. And it 'is certainly true that in the deep, winter snows not even the wolves would have heeded the sound. The snows bring Famine; and when Famine comes to keep its sentry-duty over the land, all the other forest laws are immediately forgotten or ignored. The pack forgets all its knowledge of the deadliness of men in the starving times.

The grouse heard the sound, and, silly creatures that they are, even they raised their heads for a single instant from their food. The felines--the great, tawny mountain lions and their smaller cousins, the lynx--all devoted at least an instant of concentrated attention to it. A raccoon, sleeping in a pine, opened its eyes, and a lone bull elk, such as some people think is beyond all other things the monarch of the forest, rubbed his neck against a tree trunk and wondered.

But yet there remained two of the larger forest creatures that did not heed at all. One was Urson, the porcupine, whose stupidity is beyond all measuring. He was too slow and patient and dull to give attention to a rifle bullet. And the other was Graycoat the coyote, gray and strange and foam-lipped, on the hillside. Graycoat could hear nothing but strange whinings and voices that rang ever in his ears. All other sounds were obscured. The reason was extremely simple. In the dog days a certain malady sometimes comes to the wild creatures, and it is dreaded worse than drought or cold or any of the manifold terrors of their lives. No one knows what name they have for this sickness. Human beings call it hydrophobia. And the coyotes are particularly susceptible to it.

Ordinarily the name of coyote is, among the beasts, a synonym for cowardice as well as a certain kind of detested cunning. All the cowardice of a mountain lion and a wolf and a lynx put together doesn't equal the amount that Graycoat carried in the end of his tail.

That doesn't mean timidity. Timidity is a trait of the deer, a gift of nature for self-preservation, and no one holds it against them. In fact, it makes them rather appealing. Cowardice is a lack of moral courage to remain and fight when nature has afforded the necessary weapons to fight with. It is sort of a betrayal of nature,--a misuse of powers. No one calls a rabbit a coward because it runs away. A warlike rabbit is something that no man has ever seen since the beginning of the world, and probably never will. Nature hasn't given the little animal any weapons.

But this is not true of the wolf or cougar. A wolf has ninety pounds of lightning-quick muscles, and teeth that are nothing but a set of very well-sharpened and perfectly arranged daggers. A cougar not only has fangs, but talons that can rend flesh more terribly than the cogs of a machine, and strength to make the air hum under his paw as he strikes it down. And so it is an extremely disappointing thing to see either of these animals flee in terror from an Airedale not half their size,--a sight that most mountain men see rather often. The fact that they act with greater courage in the famine times, and that either of them will fight to the very death when brought to bay, are not extenuating circumstances to their cowardice. A mouse will bite the hand that picks it up if it has no other choice.

A coyote is, at least in a measure, equipped for fighting. He is smaller than a wolf, and his fangs are almost as terrible. Yet a herd of determined sheep, turning to face him, puts him in a panic. The smallest dog simply petrifies him with terror. And a rifle report,--he has been known to put a large part of a county between himself and the source of the sound in the shortest possible time. If a mountain man feels like fighting, he simply calls another a coyote. It is more effective than impugning the virtue of his female ancestors. To be called a coyote means to be termed the lowest, most despised creature of which the imagination can conceive.

And besides being a perfect, unprincipled coward, he is utterly without pride. And that is saying a great deal. Most large animals have more pride than they have intelligence, particularly the bear and the moose. A mature bear, dying before his foes, will often refrain from howling even in the greatest agony. He is simply too proud. A moose greatly dislikes to appear to run away in the presence of enemies. He will walk with the dignity of a bishop until he thinks the brush has obscured him; and then he will simply fly! And there was a dog once, long ago, which, meeting on the highways a dog that was much larger and that could not possibly be mastered, would simply turn away his eyes and pretend not to see him.

A coyote is wholly without this virtue, as well as most of the other virtues of the animal world. He not only eats carrion--because if one started to condemn all the carrion-eating animals of the forest he would soon have precious few of them left--but he also eats old shoes off rubbish piles. Unlike the wolf, he does not even find his courage in the famine times. He has cunning, but cunning is not greatly beloved in men or beasts. Most folk prefer a kindly, blundering awkwardness, a simplicity of heart and spirit, such as are to be found in Woof the bear.

But Graycoat has one tendency that makes all the other forest creatures regard him with consternation: he is extremely hable to madness. Along in dog days he is seen suddenly to begin to rush through the thickets, barking and howling and snapping at invisible enemies, with foam dropping from his terrible lips. His eyes grow yellow and strange. And this is the time that even the bull elk turns off his trail. No one cares to meet Graycoat when the hydrophobia is upon him. At such time all his cunning and his terror are quite forgotten in his agony, and he is likely to make an unprovoked charge on Woof himself.

Now Graycoat came walking stiff-legged down through the thickets. And the forest creatures, from the smallest to the great, forgot the far-off peal of the rifle bullets to get out of his way.

VI

Dan and Lennox started together up the long slope of the ridge, Dan alone was armed; Lennox went with him solely as a guide. The deer season had just opened, and it might be that Dan would want to procure one of these creatures.

"But I'm not sure I want to hunt deer," Dan told him. "You speak of them as being so beautiful--"

"They are beautiful, and your grandfather would never hunt them either, except for meat. But maybe you'll change your mind when you see a buck. Besides, we might run into a lynx or a panther. But not very likely, without dogs."

They trudged up, over the carpet of pine needles. They fought their way through a thicket of buckbrush. Once they saw the gray squirrels in the tree tops. And before Lennox had as much as supposed they were near the haunts of big game, a yearling doe sprang up from its bed in the thickets.

For an instant she stood motionless, presenting a perfect target. It was evident that she had heard the sound of the approaching hunters, but had not as yet located or identified them with her near-sighted eyes. Lennox whirled to find Dan standing very still, peering along the barrel of his rifle. But he didn't shoot. A light danced in his eyes, and his fingers crooked nervously about the trigger, but yet there was no pressure. The deer, seeing Lennox move, leaped into her terror-pace,--that astounding run that is one of the fastest gaits in the whole animal world. In the wink of an eye, she was out of sight.

"Why didn't you shoot?" Lennox demanded.

"Shoot? It was a doe, wasn't it?"

"Good Lord, of course it was a doe! But there are no game laws that go back this far. Besides--you aimed at it."

"I aimed just to see if I could catch it through my sights. And I could. My glasses sort of made it blur--but I think--perhaps--that I could have shot it. But I'm not going to kill does. There must be some reason for the game laws, or they wouldn't exist."

"You're a funny one. Come three thousand miles to hunt and then pass up the first deer you see. You could almost have been your grandfather, to have done that. He thought killing a deer needlessly was almost as bad as killing a man. They are beautiful things, aren't they?"

Dan answered him with startling emphasis. But the look that he wore said more than his words.

They trudged on, and Lennox grew thoughtful. He was recalling the picture that he had seen when he had whirled to look at Dan, immediately after the deer had leaped from its bed. It puzzled him a little. He had turned to find the younger man in a perfect posture to shoot, his feet placed in exactly the position that years of experience had taught Lennox was correct; and withal, absolutely motionless. Of all the many things to learn in the wilderness, to stand perfectly still in the presence of game is one of the hardest. The natural impulse is to start,--a nervous reflex that usually terrifies the game. The principle of standing still is, of course, that it takes a certain length of time for the deer to look about after it makes its first leap from its bed, and if the hunter is motionless, the deer is usually unable to identify him as a thing to fear. It gives a better chance for a shot. What many hunters take years to learn, Dan had seemed to know by instinct. Could it be, after all, that this slender weakling, even now bowed down with a terrible malady, had inherited the true frontiersman's instincts of his ancestors?

Then all at once Lennox halted in his tracks, evidently with no other purpose than to study the tall form that now was walking up the trail in front of him. And he uttered a little exclamation of amazement.

"Listen, Dan!" he cried suddenly. "Haven't you ever been in the woods before?"

Dan turned, smiling. "No. What have I done now?"

"What have you done? You're doing something that I never saw a tenderfoot do in my life, before. I've known men to hunt for years--literally years--and not know how to do it. And that is--to place your feet."

"Place my feet? I'm afraid I don't understand."

"I mean--to walk silently. To stalk, damn it, Dan! This brush is dry. It's dry as tinder. A cougar can get over it like so much smoke, and a man who's lived all his life in the hills can usually climb a ridge and not make any more noise than a young avalanche. Just now I had a feeling that I wasn't hearing you walk, and I thought my ears must be going back on me. I stopped to see. You were doing it, Dan. You were stalking--putting down your feet like a cat. It's the hardest thing to learn there is, and you're doing it the first half-hour."

Dan laughed, delighted more than he cared to show. "Well, what of it?" he asked.

"What of it? That's it--what of it. And what caused it, and all about it. Go on and let me think."

The result of all this thought was at least to hover in the near vicinity of a certain conclusion. That conclusion was that at least a few of the characteristics of his grandfather had been passed down to Dan. It meant that possibly, if time remained, he would not turn out such a weakling, after all. Of course his courage, his nerve, had yet to be tested; but the fact remained that long generations of frontiersmen ancestors had left this influence upon him. The wild was calling to him, wakening instincts long smothered in cities, but sure and true as ever. It was the beginning of regeneration. Voices of the long past were speaking to him, and the Failings once more had begun to run true to form. Inherited tendencies were in a moment changing this weak, diseased youth into a frontiersman and wilderness inhabitant such as his ancestors had been before him.

But before ever Lennox had a chance to think all around the subject, to actually convince himself that Dan really was a throwback and recurrence of type, there ensued on that gaunt ridge a curious adventure. The test of nerve and courage was nearer than either of them had guessed.

They were slipping along over the pine needles, their eyes intent on the trail ahead. And then Lennox saw a curious thing. He beheld Dan suddenly stop in the trail and turn his eyes towards a heavy thicket that lay perhaps one hundred yards to their right. For an instant he looked almost like a wild creature himself. His head was lowered, as if he were listening. His muscles were set and ready.

Lennox had prided himself that he had retained all the powers of his five senses, and that few men in the mountains had keener ears than he. Yet it was truth that at first he only knew the silence, and the stir and pulse of his own blood. He assumed then that Dan was watching something that from his position, twenty feet behind, he could not see. He tried to probe the thickets with his eyes.

Then Dan whispered. Ever so soft a sound, but yet distinct in the silence. "There's something living in that thicket."

Then Lennox heard it too. As they stood still, the sound became ever clearer and more pronounced. Some living creature was advancing toward them; and twigs were cracking beneath its feet. The sounds were rather subdued, and yet, as the animal approached, both of them instinctively knew that they were extremely loud for the usual footsteps of any of the wild creatures.

"What is it?" Dan asked quietly.

Lennox was so intrigued by the sounds that he was not even observant of the peculiar, subdued quality in Dan's voice. Otherwise, he would have wondered at it. "I'm free to confess I don't know," he said. "It's booming right towards us, like most animals don't care to do. Of course it may be a human being. You must watch out for that."

They waited. The sound ended. They stood straining for a long moment without speech.

"That was the damndest thing!" Lennox went on. "Of course it might have been a bear--you never know what they're going to do. It might have got sight of us and turned off. But I can't believe that it was just a deer--"

But then his words chopped squarely off in his throat. The plodding advance commenced again. And the next instant a gray form revealed itself at the edge of the thicket.

It was Graycoat, half-blind with his madness, and desperate in his agony.

There was no more deadly thing in all the hills than he. Even the bite of a rattlesnake would have been welcomed beside his. He stood a long instant, and all his instincts and reflexes that would have ordinarily made him flee in abject terror were thwarted and twisted by the fever of his madness. He stared a moment at the two figures, and his red eyes could not interpret them. They were simply foes, for it was true that when this racking agony was upon him, even lifeless trees seemed foes sometimes. He seemed eerie and unreal as he gazed at them out of his burning eyes; and the white foam gathered at his fangs. And then, wholly without warning, he charged down at them.

He came with unbelievable speed. The elder Lennox cried once in warning and cursed himself for venturing forth on the ridge without a gun. He was fully twenty feet distant from Dan; yet he saw in an instant his only course. This was no time to trust their lives to the marksmanship of an amateur. He sprang towards Dan, intending to wrench the weapon from his hand.

But he didn't achieve his purpose. At the first step his foot caught in a projecting root, and he was shot to his face on the trail. But a long life in the wilderness had developed Lennox's reflexes to an abnormal degree; many crises had taught him muscle and nerve control; and only for a fraction of an instant, a period of time that few instruments are fine enough to measure, did he lie supinely upon the ground. He rolled on, into a position of defense. But he knew now he could not reach the younger man before the mad coyote would be upon them. The matter was out of his hands. Everything depended on the aim and self-control of the tenderfoot.

And at the same instant he wondered, so intensely that all other mental processes were subjugated to it, why he had not heard Dan shoot.

He looked up, and the whole weird picture was thrown upon the retina of his eyes. The coyote was still racing straight toward Dan, a gray demon that in his madness was more terrible than any charging bear or elk. For there is an element of horror about the insane, whether beasts or men, that cannot be denied. Both men felt it, with a chill that seemed to penetrate clear to their hearts. The eyes flamed, the white fangs of Graycoat caught the sunlight. And Dan stood erect in his path, his rifle half raised to his shoulder; and even in that first frenzied instant in which Lennox looked at him, he saw there was a strange impassiveness, a singular imperturbability on his face.

"Shoot, man!" Lennox shouted. "What are you waiting for?"

But Dan didn't shoot. His hand whipped to his face, and he snatched off his thick-lensed glasses. The eyes that were revealed were narrow and deeply intent. And by now, the frenzied coyote was not fifty feet distant.

All that had occurred since the animal charged had possibly taken five seconds. Sometimes five seconds is just a breath; but as Lennox waited for Dan to shoot, it seemed like a period wholly without limit. He wondered if the younger man had fallen into that strange paralysis that a great terror sometimes imbues. "Shoot!" he screamed again.

But it is doubtful if Dan even heard his shout. At that instant his gun slid into place, his head lowered, his eyes seemed to burn along the glittering barrel. His finger pressed back against the trigger, and the roar of the report rocked through the summer air.

The gun was of large caliber; and no living creature could stand against the furious, shocking power of the great bullet. The lead went straight home, full through the neck and slanting down through the breast, and the coyote recoiled as if an irresistible hand had smitten him. It is doubtful if there was even a muscular quiver after Graycoat struck the ground, not twenty feet from where Dan stood. And the rifle report echoed back to find only silence.

Lennox got up off the ground and moved over toward the dead coyote. He looked a long time at the gray body. And then he stepped back to where Dan waited on the trail.

"I take it all back," he said simply. You take what back?" What I thought about you--that the Failing line had gone to the dogs. I'll never call you a tenderfoot again."

"You are very kind," Dan answered. He looked rather tired, but was wholly unshaken. For an instant Lennox looked at his eyes and his steady hands.

"But tell me one thing," Lennox asked. "I saw the way you looked down the barrel. I could see how firm you held the rifle--the way you kept your head. And that is all like your grandfather. But why, when you had a repeating rifle, did you wait so long to shoot?"

"I just had one cartridge in my gun. I fired nine times back at the trees and only reloaded once. I didn't think of it until the coyote charged."

Lennox's answer was the last thing in the world to be expected. He opened his straight mouth and uttered a great, boyish yell of joy. His eyes seemed to light. It is a phenomenon that is ever so much oftener imagined than really seen; but the sudden, elated sparkle that came in those gray orbs was past denial. The eyes of the two men met, and Lennox shook him by the shoulder.

"You're not Dan Failing's grandson--you're Dan Failing himself!" he shouted. "No one but him would have had the self-control to wait till the game was almost on top of him--no one but him would have kept his head in a time like this. You're Dan Failing himself, I tell you, come back to earth. Grandson nothing! You're a throwback, and now you've got those glasses off, I can see his eyes looking right out of yours. Step on 'em, Dan. You'll never need 'em again. And give up that idea of dying in four months right now; I'm going to make you live. We'll fight that disease to a finish--and win!"

And that is the way that Dan Failing came into his heritage in the land of his own people, and in which a new spirit was born in him to fight--and win--and live.

BOOK TWO

THE DEBT

September was at its last days on the Umpquaw Divide,--that far wilderness of endless, tree-clad ridges where Dan Failing had gone for his last days. September, in this place, was a season all by itself. It wasn't exactly summer, because already a little silver sheath of ice formed on the lakes in the morning; and the days were clamping down in length so fast that Whisperfoot the cougar had time for a dozen killings in a single night. Fall only begins when the rains start; and there hadn't been a trickle of rain since

April. It was rather a cross between the two seasons,--the rag-tail of summer and the prelude of fall.

It was true that the leaves were shedding from the underbrush. They came yellow and they came red, and the north wind, always the first breath of winter, blew them in all directions. They made a perfect background for the tawny tints of Whisperfoot, and quite often the near-sighted deer would walk right up to him without detecting him. But the cougar always saw to it they didn't do it a second time.

It had been a particularly bad season for Whisperfoot, and he was glad that his luck had changed. The woods were so dry from the long drought that even he--and as all men know, he is one of the most silent creatures in the wilderness when he wants to be, which are the times that he doesn't want to make as much noise as a steam engine--found it hard to crawl down a deer trail without being heard. The twigs would sometimes crack beneath his feet, and this is a disgrace with any cougar. Their first lessons are to learn to walk with silence.

Woof the bear loved this month above all others. It wasn't that he needed protective coloring. He was not a hunter at all, except of grubs and berries and such small fry. He had a black coat and a clumsy stride; and he couldn't have caught a deer if his life had depended upon it. But he did like to shuffle through the fallen leaves and make beds of them in the warm afternoons; and besides, the berries were always biggest and ripest in September. The bee trees were almost full of honey. Even the fat beetles under the stumps were many and lazy.

Everywhere the forest people were preparing for the winter that would fall so quickly when these golden September days were done.

The Under Plane of the forest--those smaller peoples that live in the dust and have beautiful, tropical forests in the ferns--found themselves digging holes and filling them with stores of food. Of course they had no idea on earth why they were doing it, except that a quiver at the end of their tails told them to do so; but the result was entirely the same. They would have a shelter for the winter. Certain of the birds were beginning to wonder what the land was like to the south, and now and then waking up in the crisp dawns with decided longings for travel. The young mallards on the lakes were particularly restless, and occasionally a long flock of them would rise in the morning from the blue waters with a glint of wings,--and quite fail to come back. And one night all the forest listened to the wail of the first flock of south-going geese. But the main army of waterfowl would of course not pass until fall came in reality.

But the most noticeable change of all, in these last days of summer, was a distinct tone of sadness that sounded throughout the forest. Of course the wilderness note is always somewhat sad; but now, as the leaves fell and the grasses died, it seemed particularly pronounced. All the forest voices added to it,--the wail of the geese, the sad fluttering of fallen leaves, and even the whisper of the north wind. The pines seemed darker, and now and then gray clouds gathered, promised rain, but passed without dropping their burdens on the parched hillsides. Of course all the tones and voices of the wilderness sound clearest at night--for that is the time that the forest really comes to life--and Dan Failing, sitting in front of Lennox's house, watching the late September moon rise over Bald Mountain, could hear them very plainly.

It was true that in the two months he had spent in the mountains he had learned to be very receptive to the voices of the wilderness. Lennox had not been mistaken in thinking him a natural woodsman. He had imagination and insight and sympathy; but most of all he had a heritage of wood lore from his frontiersmen ancestors. Two months before he had been a resident of cities. Now the wilderness had claimed him, body and soul.

These had been rare days. At first he had to limit his expeditions to a few miles each day, and even then he would come in at night staggering from weariness. He climbed hills that seemed to tear his diseased lungs to shreds. Lennox wouldn't have been afraid, in a crisis, to trust his marksmanship now. He had the natural cold nerve of a marksman, and one twilight he brought the body of a lynx tumbling through the branches of a pine at a distance of two hundred yards. A shotgun is never a mountaineer's weapon--except a sawed-off specimen for family contingencies--yet Dan acquired a certain measure of skill at small game hunting, too. He got so he could shatter a grouse out of the air in the half of a second or so in which its bronze wings glinted in the shrubbery; and when a man may do this a fair number of times out of ten, he is on the straight road toward greatness.

Then there came a day when Dan caught his first steelhead in the North Fork. There was no finer sport in the whole West than this,--the play of the fly, the strike, the electric jar that carries along the line and through the arm and into the soul from where it is never quite effaced, and finally the furious strife and exultant throb when the fish is hooked. There is no more beautiful thing in the wilderness world than a steelhead trout in action. He simply seems to dance on the surface of the water, leaping again and again, and racing at an unheard-of speed down the ripples. He weighs only from three to fifteen pounds. But now and again amateur fishermen without souls have tried to pull him in with main strength, and are still somewhat dazed by the result. It might be done with a steel cable, but an ordinary line or leader breaks like a cobweb. When his majesty the steelhead takes the fly and decides to nm, it can be learned after a time that the one thing that may be done is to let out all the line and with prayer and nimbleness try to keep up with him.

Dan fished for lake trout in the lakes of the plateau; he shot waterfowl in the tule marshes; he hunted all manner of living things with his camera. But most of all he simply studied, as his frontiersmen ancestors had done before him. He found unceasing delight in the sagacity of the bear, the grace of the felines, the beauty of the deer. He knew the chipmunks and the gray squirrels and the snowshoe rabbits. And every day his muscles had hardened and his gaunt frame had filled out.

He no longer wore his glasses. Every day his eyes had strengthened. He could see more clearly now, with his unaided eyes, than he had ever seen before with the help of the lens. And the moonlight came down through a rift in the trees and showed that his face had changed too. It was no longer so white. The eyes were more intent. The lips were straighter.

"It's been two months," Silas Lennox told him, "half the four that you gave yourself after you arrived here. And you're twice as good now as when you came."

Dan nodded. "Twice! Ten times as good! I was a wreck when I came. To-day I climbed halfway up Baldy--within a half mile of Snowbird's cabin--without stopping to rest."

Lennox looked thoughtful. More than once, of late, Dan had climbed up toward Snowbird's cabin. It was true that his guest and his daughter had become the best of companions in the two months; but on second thought, Lennox was not in the least afraid of complications. The love of the mountain women does not go out to physical inferiors. "Whoever gets her," he had said, "will have to tame her," and his words still held good. The mountain women rarely mistook a maternal tenderness for an appealing man for love. It wasn't that Dan was weak except from the ravages of his disease; but he was still a long way from Snowbird's ideal.

And the explanation was simply that life in the mountains gets down to a primitive basis, and its laws are the laws of the cave. Emotions are simple and direct, dangers are real, and the family relations have remained unchanged since the first days of the race. Men do not woo one another's wives in the mountains.

There is no softness, no compromise: the male of the species provides, and the female keeps the hut. It is good, the mountain women know, when the snows come, to have a strong arm to lean upon. The man of strong muscles, of quick aim, of cool nerve in a crisis is the man that can be safely counted on not to leave a youthful widow to a lone battle for existence. Although Dan had courage and that same rigid self-control that was an old quality in his breed, he was still a long way from a physically strong man. It was still an even break whether he would ever wholly recover from his malady.

But Dan was not thinking about this now. All his perceptions had sharpened down to the finest focal point, and he was trying to catch the spirit of the endless forest that stretched in front of the house. The moon was above the pines at last, and its light was a magic. He sat breathless, his eyes intent on the silvery patches between the trees. Now and then he saw a shadow waver.

His pipe had gone out, and for a long time Lennox hadn't spoken. He seemed to be straining too, with ineffective senses, trying to recognize and name the faint sounds that came so tingling and tremulous out of the darkness. As always, they heard the stir and rustle of the gnawing people: the chipmunks in the shrubbery, the gophers who, like blind misers, had ventured forth from their dark burrows; and perhaps even the scaly glide of those mostdreaded poison people that had lairs in the rock piles.

Then, more distinct still, they heard the far-off yowl of a cougar. Yet it wasn't quite like the cougar utterances that Dan had heard on previous nights. It was not so high, so piercing and triumphant; but had rather an angry, snarling tone made up of ows and broad, nasal yahs. It came tingling up through hundreds of yards of still forest; and both of them leaned forward.

"Another deer killed," Dan suggested softly.

"No. Not this time. He missed, and he's mad about it. They often snarl that way when they miss their stroke, just like an angry cat. But listen--"

Again they heard a sound, and from some far-lying ridge, they heard a curious echo. So far it had come that only a tremor of it remained; yet every accent and intonation was perfect, and Dan was dimly reminded of some work of art cunningly wrought in miniature. In one quality alone it resembled the cougar's cry. It was unquestionably a wilderness voice,--no sound made by men or the instruments of men; and like the cougar's cry, it was simply imbued with the barbaric spirit of the wild. But while the cougar had simply yowled in disappointment, a sound wholly without rhythm or harmony, this sound was after the manner of a song, rising and falling unutterably wild and strange.

II

Dan felt that at last the wilderness itself was speaking to him. He had waited a long time to hear its voice. His thought went back to the wise men of the ancient world, waiting to hear the riddle of the universe from the lips of the Sphinx, and how he himself--more in his unconscious self, rather than conscious--had sought the eternal riddle of the wilderness. It had seemed to him that if once he could make it speak, if he could make it break for one instant its great, brooding silence, that the whole mystery and meaning of life would be in a measure revealed. He had asked questions--never in the form of words but only ineffable yearnings of his soul--and at last it had responded. The strange rising and falling song was its own voice, the articulation of the very heart and soul of the wilderness.

And because it was, it was also the song of life itself,--life in the raw, life as it is when all the superficialities that blunt the vision had been struck away. Dan had known that it would be thus. It brought strange pictures to his mind. He saw the winter snows, the spirits of Cold and Famine walking over them. He saw Fear in many guises--in the forest fire, in the landslide, in the lightning cleaving the sky. In the song were centered and made clear all the many lesser voices with which the forest had spoken to him these two months and which he had but dimly understood,--the passion, the exultation, the blood-lust, the strength, the cruelty, the remorseless, unceasing struggle for existence that makes the wilderness an eternal battle ground. But over it all was sadness. He couldn't doubt that. He heard it all too plainly. The wild was revealed to him as it never had been before.

"It's the wolf pack," Lennox told him softly. "As long as I have been in the mountains, it always hits me the same. The wolves have just joined together for the fall rutting. There's not another song like it in the whole world."

Dan could readily believe it. The two men sat still a long time, hoping that they might hear the song again. And then they got up and moved across the cleared field to the ridge beyond. The silence closed deeper around them.

"Then it means the end of the summer?" Dan asked.

"In a way, but yet we don't count the summer ended until the rains break. Heavens, I wish they would start! I've never seen the hills so dry, and I'm afraid that either Bert Cranston or some of his friends will decide it's time to make a little money fighting forest fires. Dan, I'm suspicious of that gang. I believe they've got a regular arson ring, maybe with unscrupulous stockmen behind them, and perhaps just a penny-winning deal of their own. I suppose you know about Landy Hildreth,--how he's promised to turn State's evidence that will send about a dozen of these vipers to the penitentiary?"

"Snowbird told me something about it."

"He's got a cabin over toward the marshes, and it has come to me that he's going to start to-morrow, or maybe has already started today, down into the valley to give his evidence. Of course, that is deeply confidential between you and me. If the gang knew about it, he'd never get through the thickets alive."

But Dan was hardly listening. His attention was caught by the hushed, intermittent sounds that are always to be heard, if one listens keenly enough, in the wilderness at night. "I wish the pack would sound again," he said. "I suppose it was hunting."

"Of course. And there is no living thing in these woods that can stand against a wolf pack in its full strength."

"Except man, of course."

"A strong man, with an accurate rifle, of course, and except possibly in the starving times in winter he'd never have to fight them. All the beasts of prey are out to-night. You see, Dan, when the moon shines, the deer feed at night instead of in the twilights and the dawn. And of course the wolves and the cougars hunt the deer. It may be that they are running cattle, or even sheep."

But Dan's imagination was afire. He wasn't content yet. "They couldn't be-- hunting man?" he asked.

"No. If it was midwinter and the pack was starving, we'd have to listen better. It always looked to me as if the wild creatures had a law against killing men, just as humans have. They've learned it doesn't pay--something the wolves and bear of Europe and Asia haven't found out. The naturalists say that the reason is rather simple--that the European peasant, his soul scared out of him by the government he lived under, has always fled from wild beasts. They were tillers of the soil, and they carried hoes instead of guns. They never put the fear of God into thecals and as a result there are quite a number of true stories about tigers and wolves that aren't pleasant to listen to. But our own frontiersmen were not men to stand any nonsense from wolves or cougars. They had guns, and they knew how to use them. And they were preceded by as brave and as warlike a race as ever lived on the earth-- armed with bows and arrows. Any animal that hunted men was immediately killed, and the rest found out it didn't pay."

"Just as human beings have found out the same thing--that it doesn't pay to hunt their fellow men. The laws of life as well as the laws of nations are against it."

But the words sounded weak and dim under the weight of the throbbing darkness; and Dan couldn't get away from the idea that the codes of life by which most men lived were forgotten quickly in the shadows of the pines. Even as he spoke, man was hunting man on the distant ridge where Whisperfoot had howled.

Bert Cranston, head of the arson ring that operated on the Umpquaw Divide, was not only beyond the pale in regard to the laws of the valleys, but he could have learned valuable lessons from the beasts in regard to keeping the laws of the hills. The forest creatures do not hunt their own species, nor do they normally hunt men. The moon looked down to find Bert Cranston waiting on a certain trail that wound down to the settlements, his rifle loaded and ready for another kind of game than deer or wolf. He was waiting for Landy Hildreth; and the greeting he had for him was to destroy all chances of the prosecuting attorney in the valley below learning certain names that he particularly wanted to know.

There is always a quality of unreality about a moonlit scene. Just what causes it isn't easy to explain, unless the soft blend of light and shadow entirely destroys the perspective. Old ruins will sometimes seem like great, misty ghosts of long-dead cities; trees will turn to silver; phantoms will gather in family groups under the cliffs; plain hills and valleys will become, in an instant, the misty vales of Fairyland. The scene on that distant ridge of the Divide partook of this quality to an astounding degree; and it would have made a picture no mortal memory could have possibly forgotten.

There was no breath of wind. The great pines, tall and dark past belief, stood absolutely motionless, like strange pillars of ebony. The whole ridge was splotched with patches of moonlight, and the trail, dimming as the eyes followed it, wound away into the utter darkness. Bert Cranston knelt in a brush covert, his rifle loaded and ready in his lean, dark hands.

No wolf that ran the ridges, no cougar that waited on the deer trails knew a wilder passion, a more terrible blood-lust than he. It showed in his eyes, narrow and never resting from their watch of the trail; it was in his posture; and it revealed itself unmistakably in the curl of his lips. Something like hot steam was in his brain, blurring his sight and heating his blood.

The pine needles hung wholly motionless above his head; but yet the dead leaves on which he knelt crinkled and rustled under him. Only the keenest ear could have heard the sound; and possibly in his madness, Cranston himself was not aware of it. And one would have wondered a long time as to what caused it. It was simply that he was shivering all over with hate and fury.

A twig cracked, far on the ridge above him. He leaned forward, peering, and the moonlight showed his face in unsparing detail. It revealed the deep lines, the terrible, drawn lips, the ugly hair long over the dark ears. His strong hands tightened upon the breech of the rifle. His wiry figure grew tense.

Of course it wouldn't do to let his prey come too close. Landy Hildreth was a good shot too, young as Cranston, and of equal strength; and no sporting chance could be taken in this hunting. Cranston had no intention of giving his enemy even the slightest chance to defend himself. If Hildreth got down into the valley, his testimony would make short work of the arson ring. He had the goods; he had been a member of the disreputable crowd himself.

The man's steps 'were quite distinct by now. Cranston heard him fighting his way through the brush thickets, and once a flock of grouse, frightened from their perches by the approaching figure, flew down the trail in front. Cranston pressed back the hammer of his rifle. The click sounded loud in the silence. He had grown tense and still, and the leaves no longer rustled.

His eyes were intent on a little clearing, possibly one hundred yards up the trail. The trail itself went straight through it. And in an instant more, Hildreth pushed through the buckbrush and stood revealed in the moonlight.

If there is one quality that means success in the mountains it is constant, unceasing self-control. Cranston thought that he had it. He had known the hard schools of the hills; and he thought no circumstance could break the rigid discipline in which his mind and nerves held his muscles. But perhaps he had waited too long for Hildreth to come; and the strain had told on him. He had sworn to take no false steps; that every motion he made should be cool and sure. He didn't want to attract Hildreth's attention by any sudden movement. All must be cautious and stealthy. But in spite of all these good resolutions, Cranston's gun simply leaped to his shoulder in one convulsive motion at the first glimpse of his enemy as he emerged into the moonlight.

The end of the barrel struck a branch of the shrubbery as it went up. It was only a soft sound; but in the utter silence it traveled far. But a noise in the brush might not have been enough in itself to alarm Hildreth. A deer springing up in the trail, or even a lesser creature, might make as pronounced a sound. It was true that even unaccompanied by any other suspicious circumstances, the man would have become instantly alert and watchful; but it was Extremely doubtful that his muscular reaction would have been the same. But the gun barrel caught the moonlight as it leaped, and Hildreth saw its glint in the darkness.

It was only a flash. But yet there is no other object in the material world that glints exactly like a gun barrel in the light. It has a look all its own. It is even more distinctive in the sunlight, and now and again men have owed their lives to a momentary glitter across a half-mile of forest. Of course the ordinary, peaceful, God-fearing man, walking down a trail at night, likely would not have given the gleam more than an instant's thought, a momentary breathlessness in which the throat closes and the muscles set; and it is more than probable that the sleeping senses would not have interpreted it at all. But Hildreth was looking for trouble. He had dreaded this long walk to the settlements more than any experience of his life. He didn't know why the letter he had written, asking for an armed escort down to the courts, had not brought results. But it was wholly possible that Cranston would have answered this question for him. This same letter had fallen into a certain soiled, deadly pair of hands which was the last place in the world that Hildreth would have chosen, and it had been all the evidence that was needed, at the meeting of the ring the night before, to adjudge Hildreth a merciless and immediate end. Hildreth would have preferred to wait in the hills and possibly to write another letter, but a chill that kept growing at his finger tips forbade it. And all these things combined to stretch his nerves almost to the breaking point as he stole along the moonlit trail under the pines.

A moment before the rush and whir of the grouse flock had dried the roof of his mouth with terror. The tall trees appalled him, the shadows fell upon his spirit. And when he heard this final sound, when he saw the glint that might so easily have been a gun-barrel, his nerves and muscles reacted at once. Not even a fraction of a second intervened. His gun flashed up, just as a small-game shooter hurls his weapon when a mallard glints above the decoys, and a little, angry cylinder of flame darted, as a snake's head darts, from the muzzle.

Hildreth didn't take aim. There wasn't time. The report roared in the darkness; the bullet sang harmlessly and thudded into the earth; and both of them were the last things in the world that Cranston had expected. And they were not a moment too soon. Even at that instant, his finger was closing down upon the trigger, Hildreth standing clear and revealed through the sights. The nervous response that few men in the world would be self-disciplined enough to prevent occurred at the same instant that he pressed the trigger. His own fire answered, so near to the other that both of them sounded as one report.

Most hunters can usually tell, even if they cannot see their game fall, whether they have hit or missed. This was one of the few times in his life that Cranston could not have told. He knew that as his finger pressed he had held as accurate a "bead "as at any time in his life. He did not know still another circumstance,--that in the moonlight he had overestimated the distance to the clearing, and instead of one hundreds yards it was scarcely fifty. He had held rather high. And he looked up, unknowing whether he had succeeded or whether he was face to face with the prospect of a duel to the death in the darkness.

And all he saw was Hildreth, rocking back and forth in the moonlight,--a strange picture that he was never entirely to forget. It was a motion that no man could pretend. And he knew he had not missed.

He waited till he saw the form of his enemy rock down, face half-buried in the pine needles. It never even occurred to him to approach to see if he had made a clean kill. He had held on the breast and he had a world of confidence in his great, shocking, big-game rifle. Besides, the rifle fire might attract some hunter in the hills; and there would be time in the morning to return to the body and make certain little investigations that he had in mind. And running back down the trail, he missed the sight of Hildreth dragging his wounded body, like an injured hare, into the shelter of the thickets.

III

Whisperfoot, that great coward, came out of his brush-covert when the moon rose. It was not his usual rising time. Ordinarily he found his best hunting in the eerie light of the twilight hour; but for certain reasons, his knowledge of which would be extremely difficult to explain, he let this time go by in slumber. The general verdict of mankind has decreed that animals cannot reason. Therefore it is somewhat awkward to explain how Whisperfoot knew that he needn't be in a hurry, that the moon would soon be up, and the deer would be feeding in their light. But know all these things he did, act upon them he also did, and it all came to the same in the end. Whether or not he could reason didn't affect the fact that a certain chipmunk, standing at the threshold of his house to glimpse the moonlit forest, saw him come slipping like a cloud of brown smoke from his lair a full hour after the little creature had every right to think that he had gone to his hunting,--and straightway tumbled back into his house with a near attack of heart failure.

But the truth was that the chipmunk was presuming upon his own desirability as food. His fear really wasn't justified. It would not be altogether true to say that Whisperfoot never ate chipmunks. Sometimes in winter, and sometimes in the dawns after an unsuccessful hunt, he ate things a great deal smaller and many times more disagreeable than chipmunks. But the great cat is always very proud when he first leaves his lair. He won't look at anything smaller than a horned buck. He is a great deal like a human hunter who will pass up a lone teal on the way out and slay a pair of his own live-duck decoys on the way back.

Whisperfoot had slept almost since dawn. It is a significant quality in the felines that they simply cannot keep in condition without hours and hours of sleep. It is true that they are highly nervous creatures, sensualists of the worst, and living intensely from twilight to dawn; and they burn up more nervous energy in a night than Urson, the porcupine, does in a year. In this matter of sleeping, they are in a direct contrast to the wolves, who seemingly never sleep at all, unless it is with one eye open, and in still greater contrast to the king of all beasts, the elephant, who is said to slumber less per night than that great electrical wizard whom all men know and praise.

The great eat came out yawning, as graceful a thing as treads upon the earth. He was almost nine feet long from the tip of his nose to the end of his tail, and he weighed as much as many a full-grown man. And he fairly rippled when he walked, seemingly without effort, almost without resting his cushions on the ground. He stood and yawned insolently, for all the forest world to see. He rather hoped that the chipmunk, staring with beady eyes from his doorway, did see him. He would just as soon that Woof's little son, the bear cub, should see him too. But he wasn't so particular about Woof himself, or the wolf pack whose song had just wakened him. And above all things, he wanted to keep out of the sight of men.

For when all things are said and done, there were few bigger cowards in the whole wilderness world than Whisperfoot. A good many people think that Graycoat the coyote could take lessons from him in this respect. But others, knowing how a hunter is brought in occasionally with almost all human resemblance gone from him because a cougar charged in his death agony, think this is unfair to the larger animal. And it is true that a full-grown cougar will sometimes attack homed cattle, something that no American animal cares to do unless he wants a good fight on his paws and of which the very thought would throw Graycoat into a spasm; and there have been even stranger stories, if one could quite believe them. A certain measure of respect must be extended to any animal that will hunt the great bull elk, for to miss the stroke and get caught beneath the churning, lashing, slashing, razor-edged front hoofs is simply death, painful and without delay. But the difficulty lies in the fact that these things are not done in the ordinary, rational blood of hunting. What an animal does in its death agony, or to protect its young, what great game it follows in the starving times of winter, can be put to neither its debit nor its credit. A coyote will charge when mad. A raccoon will put up a wicked fight when cornered. A hen will peck at the hand that robs her nest. When hunting was fairly good, Whisperfoot avoided the elk and steer almost as punctiliously as he avoided men, which is saying very much indeed; and any kind of terrier could usually drive him straight up a tree.

But he did like to pretend to be very great and terrible among the smaller forest creatures. And he was Fear itself to the deer. A human hunter who would kill two deer a week for fifty-two weeks would be called a much uglier name than poacher; but yet this had been Whisperfoot's record, on and off, ever since his second year. Many a great buck wore the scar of the full stroke,--after which Whisperfoot had lost his hold. Many a fawn had crouched panting with terror in the thickets at just a tawny light on the gnarled limb of a pine. Many a doe would grow great-eyed and terrified at just his strange, pungent smell on the wind.

He yawned again, and his fangs looked white and abnormally large in the moonlight. His great, green eyes were still clouded and languorous from sleep. Then he began to steal up the ridge toward his hunting grounds. Dry as the thickets were, still he seemed to traverse them with almost absolute silence. It was a curious thing that he walked straight in the face of the soft wind that came down from the snow fields, and yet there wasn't a weathercock to be seen anywhere. And neither had the chipmunk seen him wet a paw and hold it up, after the approved fashion of holding up a finger. He had a better way of knowing,--a chill at the end of his whiskers.

In fact, the other forest creatures did not see him at all. He took very great precautions that they shouldn't. Whisperfoot was not a long-distance runner, and his whole success depended on a surprise attack, either by stalking or from ambush. In this he is different from his fellow cowards, the wolves. Whisperfoot catches his meat fresh, before terror has time to steal out of the heart and poison it; and thus, he tells his cubs, he is a higher creature than the wolves. He kept to the deepest shadow, sometimes the long, strange profile of a pine, sometimes just the thickets of buckbrush.

And by now, he no longer cared to yawn. He was wide awake. The sleep had gone out of his eyes and left them swimming in a curious, blue-green fire. And the hunting madness was getting to him: that wild, exultant fever that comes fresh to all the hunting creatures as soon as the night comes down.

The little, breathless night sounds in the brush around him seemed to madden him. They made a song to him, a strange, wild melody that even such frontiersmen as Dan and Lennox could not experience. A thousand smells brushed down to him on the wind, more potent than any wine or lust. He began to tremble all over with rapture and excitement. But unlike Cranston's trembling, no wilderness ear was keen enough to hear the leaves rustling beneath him.

His excitement did not affect his hunting skill at all. In fact, he couldn't succeed without it. A human hunter, with the same excitement and fever, would have been rendered impotent long since. His aim would be shattered, he would make false steps to frighten the game, and not even Urson, the porcupine, would really have cause to fear him. The reason is rather simple. Man has lived a civilized existence for so long that many of the traits that make him a successful hunter have to be laboriously re-learned. As soon as he becomes excited, he forgets his training. The hunting cunning of a cougar, however, is inborn, and like a great pianist, he can usually do better when he is warmed up to his work.

Men would cross many seas for a few minutes of such wild, nerve-tingling rapture as Whisperfoot knew as he crept into his hunting grounds. Ever he went more cautiously, his tawny body lowering. And just as he reached the ridge top he heard his first game.

It was just a rustle in the thickets at one side. Whisperfoot stopped dead still, then slowly lowered his body. The only motion left was the sinuous whipping of his tail. But he couldn't identify his game yet. He peered with fiery eyes into the darkness. He was almost in leaping range already.

But at once he knew that the creature that grunted and stirred in the brush was not a deer. A deer would have detected his presence long since, as the animal was at one side of him, instead of in front, and would have caught his scent. Then, the wind blowing straighter, he recognized the creature. It was just old Urson, the porcupine.

For very good reasons, Whisperfoot never attacked Urson except in moments of utmost need. It was extremely doubtful that he spared him for the same reason that he was spared by the wisest of the mountaineers,--that he was game to be taken when starving and when no other could be procured. It was rather that he was very awkward to kill and considerably worse to eat.

It is better to dine on nightshade, says a forest law, than to eat a porcupine; for the former innocent-looking little berry is almost as fast a death as a rifle bullet, and the flesh of the latter animal will torture with a hundred red-hot fires in the vitals before its eater is driven to its eternal lair. But it isn't that the porcupine's flesh is poison. It is just that an incautious bite on its armored body will fill the throat and mouth with spines, needle points that work ever deeper until they result in death. And so it is quite a tribute to Whisperfoot's intelligence that he had killed and devoured no less than a dozen porcupines and still lived to tell the tale.

He simply knew how to handle them. He knew an upward scoop with the end of his claws that would tip the creature over; and then he would pounce on the unprotected abdomen. But it was considerable trouble, and he had to be careful of the spines all the time he was eating,--a particular annoyance to one who habitually and savagely bolts his food. So he made a careful detour about Urson and continued on his way. He heard the latter squealing and rattling his quills behind him.

IV

Shortly after nine o'clock, Whisperfoot encountered his first herd of deer. But they caught his scent and scattered before he could get up to them. He met Woof, grunting through the underbrush, and again he punctiliously, but with wretched spirit, left the trail. A fight with Woof the bear was one of the most unpleasant experiences that could be imagined. He had a pair of strong arms of which one embrace of a cougar's body meant death in one long shriek of pain. Of course they didn't fight often. They had entirely opposite interests. The bear was a berry-eater and a honey-grubber, and the cougar cared too much for his own life and beauty to tackle Woof in a hunting way.

A fawn leaped from the thicket in front of him, startled by his sound in the thicket. The truth was, Whisperfoot had made a wholly unjustified misstep on a dry twig, just at the crucial moment. Perhaps it was the fault of

Woof, whose presence had driven Whisperfoot from the trail, and perhaps because old age and stiffness was coming upon him. But neither of these facts appeased his anger. He could scarcely suppress a snarl of fury and disappointment.

He continued along the ridge, still stealing, still alert, but his anger increasing with every moment. The fact that he had to leave the trail again to permit still another animal to pass, and a particularly insignificant one too, didn't make him feel any better. This animal had a number of curious stripes along his back, and usually did nothing more desperate than steal eggs and eat bird fledglings. Whisperfoot could have crushed him with one bite, but this was one thing that the great cat, as long as he lived, would never try to do. He got out of the way politely when Stripe-back was still a quarter of a mile away; which was quite a compliment to the little animal's ability to introduce himself. Stripe-back was familiarly known as a skunk.

Shortly after ten, the mountain lion had a remarkably fine chance at a buck. The direction of the wind, the trees, the thickets and the light were all in his favor. It was old Blacktail, wallowing in the salt lick; and Whisperfoot's heart bounded when he detected him.

No human hunter could have laid his plans with greater care. He had to cut up the side of the ridge, mindful of the wind. Then there was a long dense thicket in which he might approach within fifty feet of the lick, still with the wind in his face. Just beside the lick was another deep thicket, from which he could make his leap.

Blacktail was wholly unsuspecting. No creature in the Oregon woods was more beautiful than he. He had a noble spread of antlers, limbs that were wings, and a body that was grace itself. He was a timid creature, but he did not even dream of the tawny Danger that this instant was creeping through the thickets upon him.

Whisperfoot drew near, with infinite caution. He made a perfect stalk clear to the end of the buckbrush. Thirty feet more--thirty feet of particularly difficult stalking--and he would be in leaping range. If he could only cross this last distance in silence, the game was his.

His body lowered. The tail lashed back and forth, and now it had begun to have a slight vertical motion that frontiersmen have learned to watch for. He placed every paw with consummate grace, and few sets of human nerves have sufficient control over leg muscles to move with such astounding, exacting patience. He scarcely seemed to move at all.

The distance slowly shortened. He was almost to the last thicket, from which he might spring. His wild blood was leaping in his veins.

But when scarcely ten feet remained to stalk, a sudden sound pricked through the darkness. It came from afar, but it was no less terrible. It was really two sounds, so close together that they sounded as one. Neither Blacktail nor Whisperfoot had any delusions about them. They recognized them at once, in strange ways under the skin that no man may describe, as the far-off reports of a rifle. Just to-day Blacktail had seen his doe fall bleeding when this same sound, only louder, spoke from a covert from which Bert Cranston had poached her,--and he left the lick in one bound.

Terrified though he was by the rifle shot, still Whisperfoot sprang. But the distance was too far. His outstretched paw hummed down four feet behind Blacktail's flank. Then forgetting everything but his anger and disappointment, the great cougar opened his mouth and howled.

Howling, the forest people know, never helped one living thing. Of course this means sudi howls as Whisperfoot uttered now, not that deliberate long singsong by which certain of the beasts of prey will sometimes throw a herd of game into a panic and cause them to run into an ambush. All Whisperfoot's howl of anger achieved was to frighten all the deer out of his territory and render it extremely unlikely that he would have another chance at them that night. Even Dan and Lennox, too far distant to hear the shots, heard the howl very plainly, and both of them rejoiced that he had missed.

The long night was almost done when Whisperfoot even got sight of further game. Once a flock of grouse exploded with a roar of wings from a thicket; but they had been wakened by the first whisper of dawn in the wind, and he really had no chance at them. Soon after this, the moon set.

The larger creatures of the forest are almost as helpless in absolute darkness as human beings. It is very well to talk of seeing in the dark, but from the nature of things, even vertical pupils may only respond to light. No owl or bat can see in absolute darkness. Although the stars still burned, and possibly a fine filament of light had spread out from the East, the descending moon left the forest much too dark for Whisperfoot to hunt with any advantage. It became increasingly likely that he would have to retire to his lair without any meal whatever.

But still he remained, hoping against hope. After a futile fifteen minutes of watching a trail, he heard a doe feeding on a hillside. Its footfall was not so heavy as the sturdy tramp of a buck, and besides, the bucks would be higher on the ridges this time of morning. He began a cautious advance toward it.

For the first fifty yards the hunt was in his favor. He came up wind, and the brush made, a perfect cover. But the doe unfortunately was standing a full twenty yards farther, in an open glade. For a long moment the tawny creature stood motionless, hoping that the prey would wander toward him. But even in this darkness, he could tell that she was making a half-circle that would miss him by forty yards, a course that would eventually take her down wind in almost the direction that Whisperfoot had come.

Under ordinary circumstances, Whisperfoot would not have made an attack. A cougar can run swiftly, but a deer is light itself. The big cat would have preferred to linger, a motionless thing in the thickets, hoping some other member of the deer herd to which the doe must have belonged would come into his ambush. But the hunt was late, and Whisperfoot was very, very angry. Too many times this night he had missed his kill. Besides, the herd was certainly somewhere down wind, and for certain very important reasons a cougar might as well hunt elephants as try to stalk down wind. The breeze carries his scent more surely than a servant carries a visiting card. In desperation, he leaped from the thicket and charged the deer.

In spite of the preponderant odds against him, the charge was almost a success. He went fully half the distance between them before the deer perceived him. Then she leaped. There seemed to be no interlude of time between the instant that she beheld the dim, tawny figure in the air and that in which her long legs pushed out in a spring. But she didn't leap straight ahead. She knew enough of the cougars to know that the great cat would certainly aim for her head and neck in the same way that a duck-hunter leads a fast-flying duck,--hoping to intercept her leap. Even as her feet left the ground she seemed to whirl in the air, and the deadly talons whipped down in vain. Then, cutting back in front, she raced down wind.

It is usually the most unmitigated folly for a cougar to chase a deer against which he has missed his stroke; and it is also quite fatal to his dignity. And whoever doubts for a minute that the larger creatures have no dignity, and that it is not very dear to them, simply knows nothing about the ways of animals. They cling to it to the death. And nothing is quite so amusing to old

Woof, the bear--who, after all, has the best sense of humor in the forest--as the sight of a tawny, majestic mountain lion, rabid and foaming at the mouth, in an effort to chase a deer that he can't possibly catch. But to-night it was too dark for Woof to see. Besides, one disappointment after another had crumbled, as the rains crumble leaves, the last vestige of Whisperfoot's self-control. Snarling in fury, he bounded after the doe.

She was lost to sight at once in the darkness, but for fully thirty yards he raced in her pursuit. And it is true that deep down in his own well of instincts--those mysterious waters that the events of life can hardly trouble--he really didn't expect to overtake her. If he had stopped to think, it would have been one of the really great surprises of his life to hear the sudden, unmistakable stir and movement of a large, living creature not fifteen feet distant in the thicket.

He didn't stop to think at all. He didn't puzzle on the extreme unlikelihood of a doe halting in her flight from a cougar. It is doubtful whether, in the thickets, he had any perceptions of the creature other than its movements. He was running down wind, so it is certain that he didn't smell it. If he saw it at all, it was just as a shadow, sufficiently large to be that of a deer. It was moving, crawling as Woof sometimes crawled, seemingly to get out of his path. And Whisperfoot leaped straight at it.

It was a perfect shot. He landed high on its shoulders. His head lashed down, and the white teeth closed. All the long life of his race he had known that pungent essence that flowed forth. His senses perceived it, a message shot along his nerves to his brain. And then he opened his mouth in a high, far-carrying squeal of utter, abject terror.

He sprang a full fifteen feet back into the thickets; then crouched. The hair stood still at his shoulders, his claws were bared; he was prepared to fight to the death. He didn't understand. He only knew the worst single terror of his life. It was not a doe that he had attacked in the darkness. It was not Urson, the porcupine, or even Woof. It was that imperial master of all things, man himself. Unknowing, he had attacked Landy Hildreth, lying wounded from Cranston's-bullet beside the trail. Word of the arson ring would never reach the settlements, after all.

And as for Whisperfoot,--the terror that choked his heart with blood began to wear off in a little while. The man lay so still in the thickets. Besides, there was a strange, wild smell in the air. Whisperfoot's stroke had gone home so true there had not even been a fight. The darkness began to lift around him, and a strange exultation, a rapture unknown before in all his hunting, began to creep into his wild blood. Then, as a shadow steals, he went creeping back to his dead.

Dan Failing had been studying nature on the high ridges; and he went home by a back trail that led to old Bald Mountain. Many a man of longer residence in the mountains wouldn't have cared to strike off through the thickets with no guide except his own sense of direction. The ridges are too many, and they look too much alike. It is very easy to walk in a great circle--because one leg tires before the other--with no hope whatever of anything except the spirit ever rising above the barrier of the pines. But Dan always knew exactly where he was. It was part of his inheritance from his frontiersmen ancestors, and it freed his wings in the hills.

The trail was just a narrow serpent in the brush; and it had not been made by gangs of laborers, working with shovels and picks. Possibly half a dozen white men, in all, had ever walked along it. It was just the path of the wild creatures, worn down by hoof and paw and cushion since the young days of the world.

It was covered, like a sheep lane, with little short triangles in the yellow dirt. Some of them were hardly larger than the print of a man's thumb, and they went all the way up to a great imprint that Dan could scarcely cover with his open hand. All manner of deer, from seasonal fawns with spotted coats and wide, startled eyes to the great bull elk, monarch of the forest, had passed that way before him. Once he found the traces of an old kill, where a cougar had dined and from which the buzzards had but newly departed. And once he saw where Woof had left his challenge in the bark of a great pine.

This is a very common thing for Woof to do,--to go about leaving challenges as if he were the most warlike creature in the world. In reality, he never fights until he is driven to it, and then his big, furry arms turned out to be steel compressors of the first order; he is patient and good-natured and ordinarily all he wants to do is sleep in the leaves and grunt and soliloquize and hunt berries. But woe to the man or beast who meets him in a rough-and-tumble fight. Unlike his great cousin the Grizzly, that American Adamzad that not only walks like a man but kills cattle like a butcher, he almost never eats meat. No one ever pays any attention to his challenges either, and likely he never thought any one would. They seemed to be the result of an inherited tendency with him, just as much as to grow drowsy in winter, or to scratch fleas from his furry hide.

He sees a tree that suits his fancy and immediately stands oil his hind legs beside it. Then he scratches the bark, just as high up as he can reach. The idea seemed to be that if any other bear should journey along that way, should find that he couldn't reach as high, he would immediately quit the territory. But it doesn't work out in practice. Nine times out of ten there wiD be a dozen Woofs in the same neighborhood, no two of equal size, yet they hunt their berries and rob their bee trees in perfect peace. Perhaps the impulse still remains, a dim, remembered instinct, long after it has outlived its usefulness,--just as man, ten thousand years after his arboreal existence, will often throw his arms into the air as if to seize a tree branch when he is badly frightened.

It was a roundabout trail home, but yet it had its advantages. It took him within two miles of Snowbird's lookout station, and at this hour of day he had been particularly fortunate in finding her at a certain spring on the mountain side. It was a rather singular coincidence. Along about four he would usually find himself wandering up that way. Strangely enough, at the same time, it was true that she had an irresistible impulse to go down and sit in the green ferns beside the same spring. They always seemed to be surprised to see one another. In reality, either of them would have been considerably more surprised had the other failed to put in an appearance. And always they had long talks, as the afternoon drew to twilight.

"But I don't think you ought to wait so late before starting home," the girl would always say. "You're not a human hawk, and it is easier to get lost than you think."

And this solicitude, Dan rightly figured, was a good sign. There was only one objection to it. It resulted in an unmistakable inference that she considered him unable to take care of himself , r--and that was the last thing on earth that he wanted her to think. He understood her weD enough to know that her standards were the standards of the mountains, valuing strength and self-reliance above all things. He didn't stop to question why, every day, he trod so many weary miles to be with her.

She was as natural as a fawn; and many times she had quite taken away his breath. And once she did it litterally. He didn't think that so long as death spared him he would ever be able to forget that experience. It was her birthday, and knowing of it in time he had arranged for the delivery of a certain package, dear to a girlish heart, at her father's house. In the trysting hour he had come trudging over the hills with it, and few experiences in his life had ever yielded such unmitigated pleasure as the sight of her, glowing white and red, as she took off its wrapping paper. It was a jolly old gift, he recollected.--And when she had seen it, she fairly leaped at him. Her warm, round arms around his neck, and the softest, loveliest lips in the world pressed his. But in those days he didn't have the strength that he had now. He felt he could endure the same experience again with no embarrassment whatever. His first impression then, besides abounding, incredible astonishment, was that she had quite knocked out his breath. But let it be said for him that he recovered with notable promptness. His own arms had gone up and closed around,--and the girl had wriggled free.

"But you mustn't do that!" she told him.

"But, good Lord, girl! You did it to me! Is there no justice in women?"

"But I did it to thank you for this lovely gift. For remembering me--for being so good--and considerate. You haven't any cause to thank me."

He had many very serious difficulties in thinking it out. And only one conclusion was obtainable,--that Snowbird kissed as naturally as she did anything else, and the kiss meant exactly what she said it did and no more. But the fact remained that he would have walked a good many miles farther if he thought there was any possibility of a repeat.

But all at once his fantasies were suddenly and rudely dispelled by the intrusion of realities. Even a man in the depths of concentration cannot be inattentive to the wild sounds of the mountains. They have a commanding, a penetrating quality all their own. A mathematician cannot walk over a mountain trail pondering on the fourth dimension when some living creature is consistently cracking brush in the thickets beside him. Human nature is directly opposed to such a thing, and it is too much to expect of any man. He has too many race memories of saber-tooth tigers, springing from their lairs, and likely he has heard too many bear stories in his youth.

Dan had been walking silently himself in the pine needles. As Lennox had wondered at long ago, he knew how by instinct; and instinctively he practiced this attainment as soon as he got out into the wild. The creature was fully one hundred yards distant, yet Dan could hear him with entire plainness. And for a while he couldn't even guess what manner of thing it might be.

A cougar that made so much noise would be immediately expelled from the union. A wolf pack, running by sight, might crack brush as freely; but a wolf pack would also bay to wake the dead. Of course it might be an elk or a steer, and still more likely, a bear. He stood still and listened. The sound grew nearer.

Soon it became evident that the creature was either walking with two legs, or else was a four-footed animal putting two feet down at the same instant. Dan had learned to wait. He stood perfectly still. And gradually he came to the conclusion that he was listening to the footfall of another man.

But it was rather hard to imagine what a man might be doing on this lonely hill. Of course it might be a deer hunter; but few were the valley sportsmen who had penetrated to this far land. The footfall was much too heavy for Snowbird. The steps were evidently on another trail that intersected his own trail one hundred yards farther up the hill. He had only to stand still, and in an instant the man would come in sight.

He took one step into the thickets, prepared to conceal himself if it became necessary.

Then he waited. Soon the man stepped out on the trail.

Even at the distance of one hundred yards, Dan had no difficulty whatever in recognizing him. He could not mistake this tall, dark form, the soiled, slouchy clothes, the rough hair, the intent, dark features. It was a man about his own age, his own height, but weighing fully twenty pounds more, and the dark, narrow eyes could belong to no one but Bert Cranston. He carried his rifle loosely in his arms.

He stopped at the forks in the trail and looked carefully in all directions. Dan had every reason to think that Cranston would see him at first glance. Only one clump of thicket sheltered him. But because Dan had learned the lesson of standing still, because his olive-drab sporting clothes blended softly with the colored leaves, Cranston did not detect him. He turned and strode on down the trail.

He didn't move quite like a man with innocent purposes. There was something stealthy, something sinister in his stride, and the way he kept such a sharp lookout in all directions. Yet he never glanced to the trail for deer tracks, as he would have done had he been hunting. Without even waiting to meditate on the matter, Dan started to shadow him.

Before one hundred yards had been traversed, he could better understand the joy the cougar takes in his hunting. It was the same process,--a cautious, silent advance in the trail of prey. He had to walk with the same caution, he had to take advantage of the thickets. He began to feel a curious excitement.

Cranston seemed to be moving more carefully now, examining the brush along the trail. Now and then he glanced up at the tree tops. And all at once he stopped and knelt in the dry shrubbery.

At first all that Dan could see was the glitter of a knife blade. Cranston seemed to be whittling a piece of dead pine into fine shavings. Now he was gathering pine needles and small twigs, making a little pile of them. And then, just as Cranston drew his match, Dan saw his purpose.

Cranston was at his old trade,--setting a forest fire.

VI

Foe two very good reasons, Dan didn't call to Cranston at once. The two reasons were that Cranston had a rifle and that Dan was unarmed. It might be extremely likely that Cranston would choose the most plausible and effective means of preventing an interruption of his crime, and by the same token, prevent word of the crime ever reaching the authorities. The rifle contained five cartridges, and only one was needed.

But the idea of backing out, unseen, never even occurred to Dan. The fire would have a tremendous headway before he could summon help. Although it was near the lookout station, every condition pointed to a disastrous fire. The brush was dry as tinder, not so heavy as to choke the wind, but yet tall enough to carry the flame into the tree tops. The stiff breeze up the ridge would certainly carry the flame for miles through the parched Divide before help could come. In the meantime stock and lives and homes would be endangered, besides the irreparable loss of timber. There were many things that Dan might do, but giving up was not one of them.

After all, he did the wisest thing of all. He simply came out in plain sight and unconcernedly walked down the trail toward Cranston. At the same instant, the latter struck his match.

As Dan was no longer stalking, Cranston immediately heard his step. He whirled, recognized Dan, and for one long instant in which the world seemed to have time in plenty to make a complete revolution, he stood perfectly motionless. The match flared in his dark fingers, his eyes-full of singular conjecturing--rested on Dan's face. No instant of the latter's life had ever been fraught with greater peril. He understood perfectly what was going on in Cranston's mind. The fire-fiend was calmly deciding whether to shoot or whether to bluff it out. One required no more moral courage than the other. It really didn't make a great deal of difference to Cranston.

He had been born in the hills, and his spirit was the spirit of the wolf,--to kiD when necessary, without mercy or remorse. Besides, Dan represented, in his mind, all that Cranston hated,--the law, gentleness, the great civilized world that spread below. But in spite of it, he decided that the killing was not worth the cartridge. The other course was too easy. He did not even dream that Dan had been shadowing him and had seen his intention. He would have laughed at the idea that a "tenderfoot" could thus walk behind him, unheard. Without concern, he scattered with his foot the little heap of kindling, and slipping his pipe into his mouth, he touched the flaring match to it. It was a wholly admirable little piece of acting, and would have deceived any one who had not seen his previous preparations. The fact that the pipe was empty mattered not one way or another. Then he walked on down the trail toward Dan.

Dan stopped and lighted his own pipe. It was a curious little truce. And then he leaned back against the great, gray trunk of a fallen tree.

"Well, Cranston," he said civilly. The men had met on previous occasions, and always there had been the same invisible war between them.

"How do you do. Failing," Cranston replied. No perceptions could be so blunt as to miss the premeditated insult in the tone. He didn't speak in his own tongue at all, the short, guttural "Howdy" that is the greeting of the mountain men. He pronounced all the words with an exaggerated precision, an unmistakable mockery of Dan's own tone. In his accent he threw a tone of sickly sweetness, and his inference was all too plain. He was simply calling Failing a milksop and a white-liver; just as plainly as if he had used the words.

The eyes of the two men met. Cranston's lips were slightly curled in an unmistakable leer. Dan's were very straight. And in one thing at least, their eyes looked just the same. The pupils of both pairs had contracted to steel points, bright in the dark gray of the irises. Cranston's looked somewhat red; and Dan's were only hard and bright.

Dan felt himself straighten; and the color mounted somewhat higher in his brown cheeks. But he did not try to avenge the insult--yet. Cranston was still fifteen feet distant, and that was too far. A man may swing a rifle within fifteen feet. The fact that they were in no way physical equals did not even occur to him. When the insult is great enough, such considerations cannot possibly matter. Cranston was hard as steel, one hundred and seventy pounds in weight. Dan did not touch one hundred and fifty, and a deadly disease had not yet entirely relinquished its hold upon him.

"I do very well, Cranston," Dan answered in the same tone. "Wouldn't you like another match? I believe your pipe has gone out."

Very little can be said for the wisdom of this remark. It was simply human,--

that age-old creed to answer blow for blow and insult for insult. Of course the inference was obvious,--that Dan was accusing him, by innuendo, of his late attempt at arson. Cranston glanced up quickly, and it might be true that his fingers itched and tingled about the barrel of his rifle. He knew what Dan meant. He understood perfectly that Dan had guessed his purpose on the mountain side. And the curl at his lips became more pronounced.

"What a smart little boy," he scorned. "Going to be a Sherlock Holmes when he grows up." Then he half turned and the light in his eyes blazed up. He was not leering now. The mountain men are too intense to play at insult very long. Their inherent savagery comes to the surface, and they want the warmth of blood upon their fingers. The voice became guttural. "Maybe you're a spy?" he asked. "Maybe you're one of those city rats--to come up and watch us, and then nm and tell the forest service. There's two things. Failing, that I want you to know."

Dan puffed at his pipe, and his eyes looked curiously bright through the film of smoke.

"I'm not interested in hearing them," he said.

"It might pay you," Cranston went on. "One of 'em is that one man's word is good as another's in a comi;--and it wouldn't do you any good to nm down and tell tales. A man can light his pipe on the mountain side without the courts being interested. The second thing is--just that I don't think you'd find it a healthy thing to do."

"I suppose, then, that is a threat?"

"It ain't just a threat." Cranston laughed harshly,--a single, grim syllable that was the most terrible sound he had yet uttered. "It's a fact. Just try it. Failing. Just make one little step in that direction. You couldn't hide behind a girl's skirts then. Why, you city sissy, I'd break you to pieces in my hands!"

Few men can make a threat without a muscular accompaniment. Its very utterance releases pent-up emotions, part of which can only pour forth in muscular expression. And anger is a primitive thing, going down to the most mysterious depths of a man's nature. As Cranston spoke, his lip curled, his dark fingers clenched on his thick palm, and he half leaned forward.

Dan knocked out his pipe on the log. It was the only sound in that whole mountain realm; all the lesser sounds were stilled. The two men stood face to face, Dan tranquil, Cranston shaken by passion.

"I give you," said Dan with entire coldness, "an opportunity to take that back. Just about four seconds."

He stood very straight as he spoke, and his eyes did not waver in the least. It would not be the truth to say that his heart was not leaping like a wild thing in his breast. A dark mist was spreading like madness over his brain; but yet he was striving to keep his thoughts clear. It was hard to do, under insult. But he knew that only by craft, by cool thinking and planning, could he even hope to stand against the brawny Cranston. He kept a remorseless control over his voice and face. Stealthily, without seeming to do so, he was setting his muscles for a spring.

The only answer to his words was a laugh,--a roaring laugh of scorn from Cranston's dark lips. In his laughter, his intent, catlike vigilance relaxed. Dan saw a chance; feeble though it was, it was the only chance he had. And his long body leaped like a serpent through the air.

Physical superior though he was, Cranston would have repelled the attack with his rifle if he had had a chance. His blood was already at the murder heat--a point always quickly reached in Cranston--and the dark, hot fumes in his brain were simply nothing more nor less than the most poisonous, bitter hatred. No other word exists. If his class of degenerate mountain men had no other accomplishment, they could hate. All their lives they practiced the emotion: hatred of their neighbors, hatred of law, hatred of civilization in all its forms. Besides, this kind of hillman habitually fought his duels with rifles. Hands were not deadly enough.

But Dan was past his guard before he had time to raise his gun. The whole attack was one of the most astounding surprises of Cranston's life. Dan's body struck his, his fists flailed, and to protect himself, Cranston was obliged to drop the rifle. They staggered, as if in some weird dance, on the trail; and their arms clasped in a clinch.

For a long instant they stood straining, seemingly motionless. Cranston's powerful body had stood up well under the shock of Dan's leap. It was a hand-to-hand battle now. The rifle had slid on down the hillside, to be caught in a clump of brush twenty feet below. Dan called on every ounce of his strength, because he knew what mercy he might expect if Cranston mastered him. The battles of the mountains were battles to the death.

They flung back and forth, wrenching shoulders, lashing fists, teeth and feet and fingers. There were no Marquis of Queensbury rules in this battle. Again and again Dan sent home his blows; but they all seemed ineffective. By now, Cranston had completely overcome the moment's advantage the other had obtained by the power of his leap. He hurled Dan from the clinch and lashed at him with hard fists.

It is a very common thing to hear of a silent fight. But it is really a more rare occurrence than most people believe. It is true that serpents will often fight in the strangest, most eerie silence; but human beings are not serpents. They partake more of the qualities of the meat-eaters,--the wolves and the felines. After the first instant, the noise of the fight aroused the whole hillside. The sound of blows was in itself notable, and besides, both of the men were howling the primordial battle cries of hatred and vengeance.

For two long minutes Dan fought with the strength of desperation, summoning at last all that mysterious reserve force with which all men are bom. But he was playing a losing game. The malady with which he had suffered had taken too much of his vigor. Even as he struggled, it seemed to him that the vista about him, the dark pines, the colored leaves of the perennial shrubbery, the yellow path were all obscured in a strange, white mist. A great wind roared in his ears,--and his heart was evidently about to shiver to pieces.

But still he fought on, not daring to yield. He could no longer parry Cranston's blows. The latter's arms went around him in one of those deadly holds that wrestlers know; and Dan struggled in vain to free himself. Cranston's face itself seemed hideous and unreal in the mist that was creeping over him. He did not recognize the curious thumping sound as Cranston's fists on his flesh. And now Cranston had hurled him off his feet.

Nothing mattered further. He had fought the best he could. This cruel beast could pounce on him at will and hammer away his life. But still he struggled. Except for the constant play of his muscles, his almost unconscious effort to free himself that kept one of Cranston's arms busy holding him down, that fight on the mountain path might have come to a sudden end. Human bodies can stand a terrific punishment; but Dan's was weakened from the ravages of his disease. Besides, Cranston would soon have both hands and both feet free for the work, and when these four terrible weapons are used at once, the issue--soon or late--can never be in doubt.

But even now, consciousness still lingered. Dan could hear his enemy's curses,--and far up the trail, he heard another, stranger sound. It was that second of acute sensibilities that usually immediately precedes unconsciousness, and he heard it very plainly. It sounded like some one running.

And then he dimly knew that Cranston was climbing from his body. Voices were speaking,--quick, commanding voices just over him. Above Cranston's savage curses another voice rang clear, and to Dan's ears, glorious beyond all human utterance.

He opened his tortured eyes. The mists lifted from in front of them, and the whole drama was revealed. It had not been sudden mercy that had driven Cranston from his body, just when his victim's falling unconsciousness would have put him completely in his power. Rather it was something black and ominous that even now was pointed squarely at Cranston's breast.

None too soon, a ranger of the hill had heard the sounds of the struggle, and had left the trysting place at the spring to come to Dan's aid. It was Snowbird, very pale but wholly self-sufficient and determined and intent. Her pistol was quite cocked and ready.

VII

Dan Failing was really not badly hurt. The quick, lashing blows had not done more than severely bruise the flesh of his face; and the mists of unconsciousness that had been falling over him were more nearly the result of his own tremendous physical exertion. Now these mists were rising.

"Go--go away," the girl was commanding. "I think you've killed him."

Dan opened his eyes to find her kneeling close beside him, but still covering Cranston with her pistol. Her hand was resting on his bruised cheek. He couldn't have believed that a human face could be as white, while life still remained, as hers was then. All the lovely tints that had been such a delight to him, the play of soft reds and browns, had faded as an afterglow fades on the snow.

Dan's glance moved with hers to Cranston. He was standing easily at a distance of a dozen feet; and except for the faintest tremble all over his body, a muscular reaction from the violence of his passion, he had entirely regained his self-composure. This was quite characteristic of the mountain men. They share with the beasts a passion of living that is wholly unknown on the plains; but yet they have a certain quality of imperturbability known nowhere else. Nor is it limited to the native-born mountaineers. No man who intimately knows a member of that curious, keen-eyed little army of naturalists and big-game hunters who go to the north woods every fall, as regularly and seemingly as inexorably as the waterfowl go in spring, can doubt this fact. They seem to have acquired from the silence and the snows an impregnation of that eternal calm and imperturbability that is the wilderness itself. Cranston wasn't in the least afraid. Fear is usually a matter of uncertainty, and he knew exactly where he stood.

It is extremely doubtful if a plainsman would have possessed this knowledge. But a plainsman has not the knowledge of life itself that the mountaineer has, simply because he does not see it in the raw. And he has not half the intimate knowledge of death, an absolute requisite of self-composure. The mountaineer knows life in its simple phases with little tradition or convention to blur the vision. Death is a very intimate acquaintance that may be met in any snowdrift, on any rocky trail; and these conditions are very deadly to any delusions that he has in regard to himself. He acquires an ability to see just where he stands, and of course that means self-possession. This quality had something to do with the remarkable record that the mountain men, such as that magnificent warrior from Tennessee, made in the late war.

Cranston knew exactly what Snowbird would do. Although of a higher order, she was a mountain creature, even as himself. She meant exactly what she said. If he hadn't climbed from Dan's prone body, she would have shot quickly and very straight. If he tried to attack either of them now, her finger would press back before he could blink an eye, and she wouldn't weep any hysterical tears over his dead body. If he kept his distance, she wouldn't shoot at all. He meant to keep his distance. But he did know that he could insult her without danger to himself. And by now his lips had acquired their old curl of scorn.

"I'll go, Snowbird," he said. "I'll leave you with your sissy. But I guess you saw what I did to him--in two minutes."

"I saw. But you must remember he's sick. Now go."

"If he's sick, let him stay in bed--and have a wet nurse. Maybe you can be that."

The lids drooped halfway over her gray eyes, and the slim finger curled more tightly about the trigger. "Oh, I wish I could shoot you, Bert!" she said. She didn't whisper it, or hiss it, or hurl it, or do any of the things most people are supposed to do in moments of violent emotion. She simply said it, and her meaning was all the clearer.

"But you can't. And I'll pound that milksop of yours to a jelly every time I see him. I'd think, Snowbird, that you'd want a man."

He started up the trail; and then she did a strange thing. "He's more of a man than you are, right now, Bert," she told him. "He'll prove it some day." Then her arm went about Dan's neck and lifted his head upon her breast; and in Cranston's plain sight, she bent and kissed him, softly, on the lips.

Cranston's answer was an oath. It dripped from his lips, more poisonous, more malicious than the venom of a snake. His late calm, treasured so much, dropped from him in an instant. His features seemed to tighten, the dark lips drew away from his teeth. No words could have made him such an effective answer as this little action of hers. And as he turned up the trail, he called down to her a name,--that most dreadful epithet that foul tongues have always used to women held in greatest scorn.

Dan struggled in her arms. The kiss on his lips, the instant before, had not called him out of his half-consciousness. It had scarcely seemed real, rather just an incident in a blissful dream. But the word called down the trail shot out clear and vivid from the silence, just as a physician's face will often leap from the darkness after the anesthesia. The whole scene in an instant became incredibly vivid,--the dark figure on the trail, the girl's white face above him, narrow-eyed and drawn-lipped, and the dark pines, silent and sad, overhead. Something infinitely warm and tender was holding him, pressing him back against a holy place that throbbed and gave him life and strength; but he knew that this word had to be answered. And only actions, not other words, could be its payment. All the voices of his body called to him to lie still, but the voices of the spirit, those higher, nobler promptings from which no man, to the glory of the breed from which he sprung, can ever quite escape, were stronger yet. He tugged upward, straining. But he didn't even have the strength to break the hold that the soft arm had about his neck.

"Oh, if I could only pull the trigger!" she was crying. "If I could only kill him--"

"Let me." he pleaded. "Give me the pistol. I'll kill him--"

And he would. There was no flinching in the gray eyes that looked up to her. She leaned forward, as if to put the weapon in his hands, but at once drew it back. And then a single sob caught at her throat. An instant later, they heard Cranston's laughter as he vanished around the turn of the trail.

For long minutes the two of them were still. The girl still held the man's head upon her breast. The pistol had fallen in the pine needles, and her nervous hand plucked strangely at the leaves of a mountain flower. To Dan's eyes, there was something trancelike, a hint of paralysis and insensibility about her posture. He had never seen her eyes like this. The light that he had always beheld in them had vanished. Their utter darkness startled him.

He sat up straight, and her arm that had been about his neck fell at her side. He took her hand firmly in his, and their eyes met.

"We must go home, Snowbird," he told her simply. "I'm not so badly hurt but that I can make it."

She nodded; but otherwise scarcely seemed to hear. Her eyes still flowed with darkness. And then, before his own eyes, their dark pupils began to contract. The hand he held filled and throbbed with life, and the fingers closed around his. She leaned toward him.

"Listen, Dan," she said quickly. "I heard--didn't you--the last thing that he said?"

"I couldn't help but hear, Snowbird."

Her other hand sought for his. "Then you heard--payment must be made. You know what I mean, Dan. Maybe you can't go on knowing the girls that live on the plains. If I were the cause of his saying it, and you were to answer--"

It seemed to Dan that some stern code the hills, unwritten except in the hearts of the children, inexorable as night, was speaking through her lips. This was no personal thing. In some dim, half-understood way, it went in to to the basic code of life.

"People must fight their own fights, here," she told him. "The laws of the con that the plains' people can appeal to are all far away. There's no one that can do it, except you. Not my father. My father can't fight your battles here, if your honor is going to stand. It's up to you, Dan. You can't pretend that you didn't hear him. Such as you are, weak and sick to be beaten to a pulp in two minutes, you alone will have to make him answer for it. I came to your aid-- and now you must come to mine."

Her fingers no longer clasped his. Strength had come back to him, and his fingers closed down until the blood went out of hers, but she was wholly unconscious of the pain. In reality, she was conscious of nothing except the growing flame in his face. It held her eyes, in passionate fascination. His pupils were contracting to little bright dots in the gray irises. The jaw was setting, as she had never seen it before.

"Do you think, Snowbird, that you'd even have to ask me?" he demanded.

"Don't you think I understand? And it won't be in your defense--only my own duty."

"But he is so strong--and you are so weak--"

"I won't be so weak forever. I never really cared much about living before. I'll try now, and you'll see--oh, Snowbird, wait and trust me: I understand everything. It's my own fight--when you kissed me, and he cried down that word in anger and jealousy, it put the whole thing on me. No one else can make him answer; no one else has the right. It's my honor, no one else's, that stands or falls."

He lifted her hand to his lips and kissed it again and again.

And for the first time he saw the tears gathering in her dark eyes. "But you fought here, didn't you, Dan?" she asked with painful slowness. "You didn't put up your arms--or try to nm away? I didn't come till he had you done, so I didn't see." She looked at him as if her whole joy of life hung on his answer.

"Fought! I would have fought till I died I But that isn't enough, Snowbird. It isn't enough just to fight, in a case like this. A man's got to win! I would have died if you hadn't come. And that's another debt that I have to pay--only that debt I owe to you!"

She nodded slowly. The lives of the mountain men are not saved by their women without incurring obligation. She attempted no barren denials. She made no effort to pretend he had not incurred a tremendous debt when she had come with her pistol. It was an unavoidable fact. A life for a life is the code of the mountains.

"Two things I must do, before I can ever dare to die," he told her soberly. "One of them is to pay you; the other is to pay Cranston for the thing he said. Maybe the chance will never come for the first of the two; only I'll pray that it will. Maybe it would be kinder to you to pray that it wouldn't; yet I pray that it will! Maybe I can pay that debt only by being always ready, always watching for a chance to save you from any danger, always trying to protect you. You didn't come in time to see the fight I made. Besides--I lost, and little else matters. And that debt to you can't be paid until sometime I fight again--for you--and win." He gasped from his weakness, but went on bravely. "I'll never be able to feel at peace, Snowbird, until I'm tested in the fire before your eyes! I want to show you the things Cranston said of me are not true--that my courage can stand the test. "It wouldn't be the same, perhaps, with an Eastern girl. Other things matter in the valleys. But I see how it is here; that there is only one standard for men and by that standard they rise or fall. Things in the mountains are down to the essentials."

He paused and struggled for strength to continue. "And I know what you said to him," he went on. "Half-unconscious as I was, I remember every word. Each word just seems to burn into me, Snowbird, and I'll make every one of them good. You said I am a better man than he, and sometime it would be proved--and it's the truth! Maybe in a month, maybe in a year. I'm not going to die from this malady of mine now, Snowbird. I've got too much to live for-- too many debts to pay. In the end, I'll prove your words to him."

His eyes grew earnest, and the hard fire went out of them. "It's almost as if you were a queen, a real queen of some great kingdom," he told her, tremulous with a great awe that was stealing over him, as a mist steals over water. "And because I had kissed your fingers, for ever and ever I was your subject, living only to fight your fights--maybe with a dream in the end to kiss your fingers again. When you bent and kissed me on that hillside--for him to see--it was the same: that I was sworn to you, and nothing mattered in my life except the service and love I could give to you. And it's more than you ever dream, Snowbird. It's all yours, for your battles and your happiness."

The great pines were silent above them, shadowed and dark. Perhaps they were listening to an age-old story, those vows of service and self-gained worth by which the race has struggled upward from the darkness.

"But I kissed you--once before," she reminded him. The voice was just a whisper, hardly louder than the stir of the leaves in the wind.

"But that kiss didn't count," he told her. "It wasn't at all the same. I loved you then, I think, but it didn't mean what it did to-day."

"And what--" she leaned toward him, her eyes full on his, "does it mean now?"

"All that's worth while in life, all that matters when everything is said that can be said, and all is done that can be done. And it means, please God, when the debts are paid, that I may have such a kiss again."

"Not until then," she told him, whispering.

"Until then, I make oath that I won't even ask it, or receive it if you should give it. It goes too deep, dearest--and it means too much."

This was their pact. Not until the debts were paid and her word made good would those lips be his again. There was no need for further words. Both of them knew. The soldier of the queen must be tried with fire, before he may return to kiss her fingers. The light burns clear in this. No instances of degeneracy, no exceptions brought to pass by thwarted nature, can affect the truth of this.

In the skies, the gray clouds were gathering swiftly, as always in the mountains. The raindrops were falling one and one, over the forest. The summer was done, and fall had come in earnest.

VIII

The rains fell unceasingly for seven days: not a downpour but a constant drizzle that made the distant ridges smoke. The parched earth seemed to smack its lips, and little rivulets began to fall and tumble over the beds of the dry streams. The Rogue and the Umpquaw flooded and the great steelhead began to ascend their smaller tributaries. Whisperfoot hunted with ease, for the wet shrubbery did not crack and give him away. The air was filled with the call of the birds of passage.

All danger of forest fire was at once removed, and Snowbird was no longer needed as a lookout on old Bald Mountain. She went to her own home, her companion back to the valley; and now that his sister had taken his place as housekeeper. Bill had gone down to the lower foothills with a great part of the live stock. Dan spent these rainy days in toil on the hillsides, building himself physically so that he might pay his debts.

It was no great pleasure, these rainy days.

He would have greatly liked to have lingered in the square mountain house, listening to the quiet murmur of the rain on the roof and watching Snowbird at her household tasks. She could, as her father had said, make a biscuit. She could also roll up sleeves over trim, brown arms and with entire good humor do a week's laundry for three hardworking men. He would have liked to sit with her, through the long afternoons, as she knitted beside the fireplace--to watch the play of her graceful fingers and perhaps, now and then, to touch her hands when he held the skeins. But none of these things transpired. He drove himself from daylight till dark, developing his body for the tests that were sure to come.

The first few days nearly killed him. He over-exercised in the chill rain, and one anxious night he developed all the symptoms of pneumonia. Such a sickness would have been the one thing needed to make the doctor's prophecy come true. But with Snowbird's aid, and numerous hot drinks, he fought it off.

She had made him go to bed, and no human memory could be so dull as to forget the little, whispered message that she gave him with his last spoonful of medicine. She said she'd pray for him, and she meant it too,--literal, entreating prayer that could not go unheard.

She was a mountain girl, and her beliefs were those of her ancestors,-- simple and true and wholly without affectation. But he hadn't relaxed thereafter. He knew the time had come to make the test. Night after night he would go to bed half-sick from fatigue, but the mornings would find him fresh. And after two weeks, he knew he had passed the crisis and was on the direct road to complete recovery.

Sometimes he cut wood in the forest: first the felling of some tall pine, then the trimming and hewing into two-foot lengths. The blisters came on his hands, broke and bled, but finally hardened into callosities. He learned the most effective stroke to hurl a shower of chips from beneath the blade. His back and limbs hardened from the handling of heavy wood--and the cough was practically gone.

Sometimes he mended fences and did other manual labor about the ranch; but not all his exercise was taken out in work. He didn't forget his friends in the forest, creatures of talon and paw and wing. He spent long days roaming the ridges and fighting through the buckbrush, and the forest yielded up its secrets, one by one. But he knew that no mortal span of years was long enough to absorb them all. Sometimes he shot ducks over the marshes; and there was no greater sport for him in the wilds than the first sight of a fine, black-pencil line upon the distant sky, the leap through the air that it made until, in an instant's flash, it evolved into a flock of mallard passing with the wind; and then the test of eye and nerve as he saw them over the sights.

His frame filled out. His face became swarthy from constant exposure. He gained in weight. A month glided by, and he began to see the first movement of the largest forest creatures down to the foothills. For not even the animals, with the exception of the hardy wolf pack, can survive if unprotected from the winter snow and cold of the high levels. The first snow sifted from the gray sky and quickly melted on the wet pine needles. And then the migration of the deer began in earnest. Before another week was done, Whisperfoot had cause to marvel where they had all gone.

One cloudy afternoon in early November found Silas Lennox cutting wood on the ridge behind his house. It was still an open question with him whether he and his daughter would attempt to winter on the Divide. Dan of course wanted to remain, yet there were certain reasons, some very definite and others extremely vague, why the prospect of the winter in the snow fields did not appeal to the mountaineer. In the first place, all signs pointed to a hard season. Although the fall had come late, the snows were exceptionally early. The duck flight was completed two weeks before its usual time, and the rodents had dug their burrows unusually deep. Besides, too many months of snow weigh heavily upon the spirit. The wolf packs sing endlessly on the ridges, and many unpleasant things may happen. On previous years, some of the cabins on the ridges below had human occupants; this winter the whole region, for nearly seventy miles across the mountains to the foothills, would be wholly deserted by human beings. Even the ranger station, twelve miles across a steep ridge, would soon be empty. Of course a few ranchers had homes a few miles beyond the river, but the wild cataracts did not freeze in the coldest of seasons, and there were no bridges. Besides, most of the more prosperous farmers wintered in the valleys. Only a few more days would the road be passable for his car; and no time must be lost in making his decision.

Once the snows came in reality, there was nothing to do but stay. Seventy miles across the uncharted ridges on snowshoes is an undertaking for which even a mountaineer has no fondness. It might be the wisest thing, after all, to load Snowbird and Dan into his car and drive down to the valleys. The fall round-up would soon be completed. Bill would return for a few days from the valleys with new equipment to replace the broken lighting system on the car, and they could avoid the bitter cold and snow that Lennox had known so long. Of course he would miss it somewhat. He had a strong man's love for the endless drifts, the crackling dawns and the hushed, winter forest wherein not even Woof or Whisperfoot dares to go abroad. He chopped at a great log and wondered what would suit him better,--the comfort and safety of the valleys or the rugged glory of the ridges.

But at that instant, the question of whether or not he would winter on the Divide was decided for him. And an instant was all that was needed. For the period of one breath he forgot to be watchful,--and a certain dread Spirit that abides much in the forest saw its chance. Perhaps he had lived too long in the mountains and grown careless of them: an attitude that is usually punished with death. He had just felled a tree, and the trunk was still attached to the stirup by a stripe of bark to which a little of the wood adhered. He struck a furious blow at it with his ax.

He hadn't considered that the tree lay on a steep slope. As the blade fell, the great trunk simply seemed to leap. Lennox leaped too, in a frenzied effort to save his life; but already the leafy bows, like the tendrils of some great amphibian, had whipped around his legs. He fell, struggling; and then a curious darkness, streaked with flame, dropped down upon him.

An hour later he found himself lying on the still hillside, knowing only a great wonderment. At first his only impulse was to go back to sleep. He didn't understand the grayness that had come upon the mountain world, his own strange feeling of numbness, of endless soaring through infinite spaces. But he was a mountain man, and that meant he was schooled, beyond all things, to keep his self-control. He made himself remember. It was the crudest work he had ever done, and it seemed to him that his brain would shiver to pieces from the effort. Yes--he had been cutting wood on the hillside, and the shadows had been long. He had been wondering whether or not they should go down to the valleys.

He remembered now: the last blow and the rolling log. He tried to turn his head to look up to the hill.

He found himself wholly unable to do it. Something wracked him in his neck when he tried to move. But he did glance down. And yes, he could turn in this direction. And he saw the great tree trunk lying twenty feet below him, wedged in between the young pines.

He was surrounded by broken fragments of limbs, and it was evident that the tree had not struck him a full blow. The limbs had protected him to some extent. No man is of such mold as to be crushed under the solid weight of the trunk and live to remember it. He wondered if this were the frontier of death,--the grayness that lingered over him. He seemed to be soaring.

He brought himself back to earth and tried again to remember. Of course, the twilight had fallen. It had been late afternoon when he had cut the tree. His hand stole along his body; and then, for the first time, a hideous sickness came upon him. His hand was warm and wet when he brought it up. The other hand he couldn't stretch at all.

The forest was silent around him, except a bird calling somewhere near the house--a full voice, rich and clear, and it seemed to him that it had a quality of distress. Then he recognized it. It was the voice of his own daughter, Snowbird, calling for him. He tried to answer her.

It was only a whisper, at first. Yet she was coming nearer; and her own voice sounded louder. "Here, Snowbird," he called again. She heard him then: he could tell by the startled tone of her reply. The next instant she was at his side, her tears dropping on his face.

With a tremendous effort of will, he recalled his speeding faculties. "I don't think I'm badly hurt," he told her very quietly. "A few ribs broken--and a leg. But we'll have to winter here on the Divide, Snowbird mine."

"What does it matter, if you live," she cried. She crawled along the pine needles beside him, and tore his shirt from his breast. He was rapidly sinking into unconsciousness. The thing she dreaded most--that his back might be broken--was evidently not true. There were, as he said, broken ribs and evidently one severe fracture of the leg bone. Whether he had sustained internal injuries that would end his life before the morning, she had no way of knowing.

At that point, the problem of saving her father's life fell wholly into her hands. It was perfectly plain that he could not aid himself in the slightest way. It was evident, also, he could not be moved, except possibly for the distance to the house. She banished all impulse toward hysteria and at once began to consider all phases of the case.

His broken body could not be carried over the mountain road to physicians in the valleys. They must be transported to the ranch. It would take them a full day to make the trip^ even if she could get word to them at once; and twenty-four hours without medical attention would probably cost her father his life. The nearest telephone was at the ranger station, twelve miles distant over a mountain trail. The telephone line to Bald Mountain, four miles off, had been disconnected when the rains had ended the peril of the forest fire.

It all depended upon her. Bill was driving cattle into the valleys, and he and his men had in use all the horses on the ranch with one exception. The remaining horse had been ridden by Dan to some distant marshes, and as Dan would shoot until sunset, that meant he would not return until ten o'clock. There was no road for a car to the ranger station, only a rough steep trail, and she remembered, with a sinking heart, that one of Bill's missions in the valley was to procure a new lighting system. By no conceivable possibility could she drive down that mountain road in the darkness. But she was somewhat relieved by the thought that in all probability she could walk twelve miles across the mountains to the ranger station in much less time than she could drive, by automobile, seventy miles down to the ranches at the foothills about the valley.

Besides, she remembered with a gladdening heart that Richards, one of the rangers, had been a student at a medical college and had taken a position with the Forest Service to regain his health. She would cross the ridge to the station, 'phone for a doctor in the valleys, and would return on horseback with Richards for such first aid as he could give. The only problem that remained was that of getting her father into the house.

He was stirring a little now. Evidently consciousness was returning to him. And then she thanked Heaven for the few simple lessons in first aid that her father had taught her in the days before his carelessness had come upon him. He had been wise enough to know that rare would be her fortune if sometime she did not have need of such knowledge.

One of his lessons had been that of carrying an unconscious human form,--a method by which even a woman may carry, for a short distance, a heavy man. It was approximately the method used in carrying wounded in No Man's Land: the body thrown over the shoulders, one arm through the fork of the legs to the wounded man's hand. Her father was not a particularly heavy man, and she was an exceptionally strong young woman. She knew at once that this problem was solved.

The hardest part was Kf ting him to her shoulders. Only by calling upon her last ounce of strength, and tugging upward with her arms, was she able to do it. But it was fairly easy, in her desperation, to carry him down the hill. What rest she got she took by leaning against a tree, the limp body still across her shoulders.

It was a distance of one hundred yards in all. No muscles but those trained by the outdoors, no lungs except those made strong by the mountain air, could have stood that test. She laid him on his own bed, on the lower floor, and set his broken limbs the best she could. She covered him up with thick, fleecy blankets, and set a bottle of whisky beside the bed. Then she wrote a note to Dan and fastened it upon one of the interior doors.

She had learned, long ago, the value of frequent rests. She did not fly at once to her long tramp. For three minutes she lay perfectly limp on the fireplace divan, resting from the exertion of carrying her father down the hill. Then she drew on her hob-nailed boots--needed sorely for the steep climb-- and pocketed her pistol. She thrust a handful of jerked venison into the pocket of her coat and lighted the lantern. The forest night had fallen, vibrant and tremulous, over the heads the dark trees when she started out.

Far away on a distant hillside, Whisperfoot the cougar howled and complained because he could find no deer.

IX

Snowbird felt very glad of her intimate, accurate knowledge of the whole region of the Divide. In her infancy the winding trails had been her playground, and long ago she had acquired the mountaineer's sixth sense for traversing them at night. She had need of that knowledge now. The moon was dim beneath thin clouds, and the lantern she carried did not promise much aid. The glass was rather smoked from previous burnings, and its flame glowed dully and threatened to go out altogether. It cast a few lame beams on the trail beneath her feet; but they perished quickly in the expanse of darkness.

She slipped into her free, swinging stride; and the last beams from the windows of the house were soon lost in the pines behind her. It was one of those silent, breathless nights with which no mountaineer is entirely unacquainted, and for a long time the only sound she could hear was her own soft tramp in the pine needles. The trees themselves were motionless. That peculiar sound, not greatly different from that of running water which the wind often makes in the pine tops, was entirely lacking. Not that she could be deceived by it,--as stories tell that certain tenderfeet, dying of thirst in the barren hills, have been. But she always liked the sound; and she missed it especially to-night.

She felt that if she would stop to listen, there would be many faint sounds in the thickets,--those little hushed noises that the wild things make to remind night-wanderers of their presence. But she did not in the least care to hear these sounds. They do not tend toward peace of mind on a long walk over the ridges.

The wilderness began at once. Whatever influence toward civilization her father's house had brought to the wilds chopped off as beneath a blade in the first fringe of pines. This is altogether, characteristic of the Oregon forests. They are much too big and too old to be tamed in any large degree by the presence of one house. No one knew this fact better than Lennox himself who, in a hard winter of four years before, had looked out of his window to find the wolf pack ranged in a hungry circle about his house. Within two hundred yards after she had passed through her father's door, she was perfectly aware that the wild was stirring and throbbing with life about her. At first she tried very hard to think of other things. But the attempt wasn't entirely a success. And before she had covered the first of the twelve miles, the sounds that from the first had been knocking at the door of her consciousness began to make an entrance.

If a person lies still long enough, he can usually hear his heart beating and the flow of his blood in his arteries. Any sound, no matter how faint, will make itself heard at last. It was this way with a very peculiar noise that crept up through the silence from the trail behind her. She wouldn't give it any heed at first. But in a very little while indeed, it grew so insistent that she could no longer disregard it.

Some living creature was trotting along on the trail behind, keeping approximately the same distance between them.

Foregoing any attempt to ignore it, she set her cool young mind to thinking what manner of beast it might be. Its step was not greatly different from that of a large dog,--except possibly a dog would have made slightly more noise. Yet she couldn't even be sure of this basic premise, because this animal, whatever it might be, had at first seemingly moved with utmost caution, but now took less care with its step than is customary with the wild denizens of the woods. A wolf, for instance, can simply drift when it wishes, and the silence of a cougar is a name. Yet unless her pursuer were a dog, which seemed entirely unlikely, it was certainly one of these two. She would have liked very much to believe the step was that of Old Woof, the bear, suddenly curious ais to what this dim light of hers might be; but she couldn't bring herself to accept the lie. Woof, except when wounded or cornered, is the most amiable creature in the Oregon woods, and it would give her almost a sense of security to have him waddling along behind her. The wolves and cougar, remembering the arms of Woof, would not be nearly so curious. But unfortunately, the black bear had never done such a thing in the memory of man, and if he had, he would have made six times as much noise. He can go fairly softly when he is stalking, but when he is obliged to trot--as he would be obliged to do to keep up with a swift-walking human figure--he cracks twigs like a rolling log. She had the impression that the animal behind had been passing like smoke at first, but wasn't taking the trouble to do it now.

The sound was a soft pat-pat on the trail,--sometimes entirely obliterated but always recurring when she began to believe that she had only fancied its presence. Sometimes a twig, rain-soaked though it was, cracked beneath a heavy foot, and again and again she heard the brush crushing and rustling as something passed through. Behind it all, a weird motif, remained the pat-pat of cushioned feet. Sometimes, when the trail was covered with soft pine needles, it was practically indistinguishable. She had to strain to hear it,--and it is not pleasing to the spirit to have to strain to hear any sound. On the bare, rain-packed earth, even untrained plainsmen's ears could not possibly doubt the reality of the sound.

The animal was approximately one hundred feet behind. It wasn't a wolf, she thought. The wolves ran in packs this season, and except in winter were more afraid of human beings than any other living creature. It wasn't a lynx-- one of those curiosity-devoured little felines that will mew all day on a trail and never dare come near. It was much too large for a lynx. The feet fell too solidly. She had already given up the idea that it could be Woof. There were no dogs in the mountains to follow at heel; and she had no desire whatever to meet Shag, the faithful hybrid that used to be her guardian in the hills. For Shag had gone to his well-deserved rest several seasons before. Two other possibilities remained. One was that this follower was a human being, the other that it was a cougar.

Ordinarily a human being is much more potentially dangerous to a woman in the hills at night than a cougar. A cougar is an abject coward and some men are not. But Snowbird felt herself entirely capable of handling any human foes. They would have no advantage over her; they would have no purpose in killing from ambush; and she trusted to her own marksmanship implicitly. While it is an extremely difficult thing to shoot at a cougar leaping from the thicket, a tall man standing on a trail presents an easy target. Besides, she had a vague sense of discomfort that if this animal were a cougar, he wasn't acting true to form. He was altogether too bold.

She knew perfectly that many times since men came to live in the pine-clad mountains they have been followed by the great, tawny cats. Curiosity had something to do with it, and perhaps less pleasing reasons. But any dreadful instincts that such a cat may have, he utterly lacks courage to obey. He has an inborn fear of men, a fear that goes down to the roots of the world, and he simply doesn't dare make an attack. It was always a rather distressing experience, but nothing ever came of it except a good tale around a fireside. But most of these episodes, Snowbird remembered, occurred either in daylight or in the dry season. The reason was obviously that in the damp woods or at night a stalking cougar cannot be perceived by human senses. Her own senses could perceive this animal all too plainly,--and the fact suggested unpleasant possibilities.

The animal on the trail behind her was taking no care at all to go silently. He was simply pat-patting along, wholly at his ease. He acted as if the fear that men have instilled in his breed was somehow missing. And that is why she instinctively tried to hurry on the trail.

The step kept pace. For a long mile, up a barren ridge, she heard every step it made. Then, as the brush closed deeper around her, she couldn't hear it at all.

She hurried on, straining to the silence. No, the sound was stopped. Could it be that the animal, fearful at last, had turned from her trail? And then for the first time a gasp that was not greatly different from a despairing sob caught at her throat. She heard the steps again, and they were in the thickets just beside her.

Two hours before Snowbird had left the house, on her long tramp to the ranger station, Dan had started home. He hadn't shot until sunset, as he had planned. The rear guard of the waterfowl--hardy birds who spent most of the winter in the Lake region and which had come south in the great flight that had been completed some weeks before--had passed in hundreds over his blind, and he had obtained the limit he had set upon himself--ten drake mallards--by four o'clock in the afternoon. If he had stayed to shoot longer, his birds would have been wasted. So he started back along a certain winding trail that led through the thickets and which would, if followed long enough, carry him to the road that led to the valleys.

He rode one of Lennox's cattle ponies, the only piece of horse-flesh that Bill had not taken to the valleys when he had driven down the livestock. She was a pretty bay, a spirited, high-bred mare that could whip about on her hind legs at the touch of the rein on her neck. She made good time along the trail. And an hour before sunset he passed the only human habitation between the marsh and Lennox's house,--the cabin that had been recently occupied by Landy Hildreth.

He glanced at the place as he passed and saw that it was deserted. No smell of wood smoke remained in the air. Evidently Landy had gone down to the settlements with his precious testimony in regard to the arson ring. Yet it was curious that no word had been heard of him. As far as Dan knew, neither the courts nor the Forest Service had taken action.

He hurried on, four miles farther. The trail entered the heavy thickets, and he had to ride slowly. It was as wild a section as could be found on the whole Divide. Once a deer leaped from the trail, and once he heard Woof grunting in the thickets. And just as he came to a little cleared space, three strange, dark birds flung up on wide-spreading wings.

He knew them at once. All mountaineers come to know them before their days are done. They were the buzzards, the followers of the dead. And what they were doing in the thicket just beside the trail, Dan did not dare to think.

Of course they might be feeding on the body of a deer, mortally wounded by some hunter. He resolved to ride by without investigating. He glanced up. The buzzards were hovering in the sky, evidently waiting for him to pass. Then, mostly to relieve a curious sense of discomfort in his own mind, he stopped his horse and dismounted.

The twilight had started to fall, and already its first grayness had begun to soften the harder lines of forest and hill. And after his first glance at the curious white heap beside the trail, he was extremely glad that it had. But there was no chance to mistake the thing. The elements and much more terrible agents had each wrought their change, yet there was grisly evidence in plenty to show what had occurred. Dan didn't doubt for an instant but that it was the skeleton of Landy Hildreth.

He forced himself to go nearer. The buzzards were almost done, and one white bone from the shoulder gave unmistakable evidence of the passage of a bullet. What had happened thereafter, he could only guess.

He got back quickly on his horse. He understood, now, why nothing had been heard of the evidence that Landy Hildreth was to turn over to the courts as to the activities of the arson ring. Some one--probably Bert Cranston himself--had been waiting on the trail. Others had come thereafter. And his lips set in his resolve to let this murder measure in the debt he had to pay Cranston.

The Lennox house seemed very silent when, almost an hour later, he turned his horse into the corral. He had rather hoped that Snowbird would be at the door to meet him. The darkness had just fallen, and all the lamps were lighted. He strode into the living room, warming his hands an instant beside the fireplace. The fire needed fuel. It had evidently been neglected for nearly an hour.

Then he called Snowbird. His voice echoed in the silent room, unanswered. He called again, then went to look for her. At the door of the dining room he found the note that she had left for him.

It told, very simply and plainly, that her father lay injured in his bed, and he was to remain and do what he could for him. She had gone for help to the ranger station.

He leaped through the rooms to Lennox's door, then went in on tiptoe. And the first thing he saw when he opened the door was the grizzled man's gray face on the pillow.

"You're home early, Dan," he said. "How many did you get?"

It was entirely characteristic. Shaggy old Woof is too proud to howl over the wounds that lay him low, and this gray old bear on the bed had partaken of his spirit.

"Good Lord," Dan answered. "How badly are you hurt?"

"Not so bad but that I'm sorry that Snowbird has gone drifting twelve miles over the hills for help. It's dark as pitch."

And it was. Dan could scarcely make out the outline of the somber ridges against the sky.

They talked on, and their subject was whether Dan should remain to take care of Lennox, or whether he should attempt to overtake Snowbird with the horse. Of course the girl had ordered him to stay. Lennox, on the other hand, said that Dan could not help him in the least, and desired him to follow the girl.

"I'm not often anxious about her," he said slowly. "But it is a long walk through the wildest part of the Divide. She's got nothing but a pistol and a lantern that won't shine. Besides--I've had bad dreams."

"You don't mean--" Dan's words came hard--" that she's in any danger from the animals--the cougars--or the wolves?"

"Barring accidents, no. But, Dan--I want you to go. I'm resting fairly easily, and there's whisky on the table in case of a pinch. Someway--I can 't bar accidents to-night. I don't like to think of her on those mountains alone."

And remembering what had lain beside the trail, Dan felt the same. He had heard, long ago, that any animal that has once tasted human flesh loses its fear of men and is never to be trusted again. Some wild animal that still hunted the ridges had, in the last month, done just that thing. He left the room and walked softly to the door.

The night lay silent and mysterious over the Divide. He stood listening. The girl had started only an hour before, and it was unlikely that she could have traversed more than two miles of the steep trail in that time. He could fancy her toiling ever upward, somewhere on the dark ridge that lay beyond. Although the horse ordinarily did not climb a hill more swiftly than a human being, he didn't doubt but that he could overtake her before she went three miles farther. But where lay his duty,--with the injured man in the house or with the daughter on her errand of mercy in the darkness?

Then the matter was decided for him. So faint that it only whispered at the dim, outer frontiers of hearing, a sound came pricking through the darkness.

Only his months of listening to the faint sounds of the forest, and the incredible silence of the night enabled him to hear it at all. But he knew what it was, the report of a pistol. Snowbird had met an enemy in the darkness.

He called once to Lennox, snatched the shotgun that still stood where he had placed it in the corner of the room, and hastened to the corral. The mare whickered plaintively when he took her from her food.

Even in the darkest night, there is one light that never brings hope or cannot lead. It is not a twinkling, joyous light like that mysterious will-o'-the-wisp that now and again has lured travelers into the marshes to their death. Nor can any one ever mistake it, or be soothed and cheered by it. It always appears the same way,--two green circles, close together, in the darkness.

When Snowbird first heard the step in the thickets beside her, she halted bravely and held her lantern high. She understood at last. The very extremity of the beams found a reflection in two very curious circles of greenish fire: a fire that was old upon the world before man ever rubbed two sticks together to strike a flame. Of course the dim rays had simply been reflected on the eyes of some great beast of prey.

She identified it at once. Only the eyes of the felines, with vertical pupils, have this identical greenish glare. The eyes of the wolves glow in the darkness, but the circles are usually just bright points. Of course it was a cougar.

She didn't cry out again. Realizing at last the reality of her peril, her long training in the mountains came to her aid. That did not mean she was not truly and terribly afraid. The sight of the eyes of a hunting animal in the darkness calls up memories from the germplasm,--deep-buried horrors of thousands of generations past, when such lights glowed all about the mouth of the cave. Besides, the beast was hunting her. She couldn't doubt this fact. Curiosity might make a lion follow her, but it would never beget such a wild light of madness in his eyes as this she had just seen. Only the frenzied pulse of wild blood through the fine vessels of the corneas could occasion such a glow as this. She simply clamped down all her moral strength on her rising hysteria and looked her situation in the face. Her hand flew instinctively to her side, and the pistol leaped in the lantern light.

But the eyes had already blinked out before she could raise the weapon. She shot twice. The echoes roared back, unbelievably loud in the silence, and then abruptly died; and the only sound was a rustling of leaves as the cougar crouched. She sobbed once, then hurried on.

She was afraid to listen at first. She wanted to believe that her pistol fire would frighten the animal from her trail. She knew, under ordinary conditions, that it would. If he still followed, it could mean but one thing,--that some unheard-of incident had occurred to destroy his fear of men. It would mean that he had knowingly set upon her trail and was hunting her with all the age-old remorselessness that is the code of the mountains.

For a little while all was silence. Then out of the hush the thickets suddenly crashed and shook on the opposite side of the trail. She fired blindly into the thicket. Then she caught herself with a sob. But two shells remained in her pistol, and they must be saved for the test.

Whisperfoot the cougar, remembering the lessons of his youth, turned from the trail when he had first heard Snowbird's step. He had crouched and let her pass. She was walking into the wind; and as she was at the closest point a message had blown back to him.

The hair went straight on his shoulders and along his spine. His blood, running cold an instant before from fear, made a great leap in his veins. A picture came in his dark mind: the chase for a deer when the moon had set, the stir of a living thing that broke twigs in the thickets, and the leap he had made. There had been blood, that night,--the wildness and the madness and the exultation of the kill. Of course there had been terror first, but the terror had soon departed and left something lying warm and still in the thickets. It was the same game that walked his trail in front--game that died easily and yet, in a vague way he did not understand, the noblest game of all. It was living flesh, to tear with talon and fang.

All his training, all the instincts imbued in him by a thousand generations of cougars who knew this greatest fear, were simply obliterated by the sudden violence of his hunting-madness. He had tasted this blood once, and it could never be forgotten. The flame leaped in his eyes. And then he began the stalk.

A cougar, trying to creep silently on its game, does not move quickly. It simply steals, as a serpent steals through the grass. Whisper foot stalked for a period of five minutes, to learn that the prey was farther away from him at every step.

He trotted forward until he came close, and again he stalked. Again he found, after a few minutes of silent creeping through the thickets, that he had lost distance. Evidently this game did not feed slowly, like the deer. It was to be a chase then. Again he trotted within one \[hundred feet of the girl. i

Three times more he tried to stalk before he finally gave it up altogether. This game was like the porcupine,--simply to be chased down and taken. As in the case of all animals that hunt their game by overtaking it, there was no longer any occasion for going silently. The thing to do was to come close and spring from the trail behind.

Though the fear was mostly gone, the cougar retained enough of that caution that most wild animals exhibit when hunting a new game so that he didn't attempt to strike Snowbird down at once. But as the chase went on, his passion grew upon him. Ever he crept nearer. And at last he sprang full into the thickets beside her.

At that instant she had shot for the first time. Because the light had left his eyes before she could find aim, both shots had been clean misses. And terrible as the reports were, he was too engrossed in the chase to be frightened away by mere sound. This was the cry the manpack always made,--these sudden, startling sounds in the silence. But he felt no pain. He crouched a moment, shivering. Then he bounded on again.

The third shot was a miss too; in fact, there had been no chance for a hit. A sound in the darkness is as unreliable a target as can possibly be imagined. And it didn't frighten him as much as the others.

Three times he crouched, preparing for a spring, and three tunes his tawny tail began that little up-and-down motion that is always the warning before his leap. But each time, as he waited to find his courage, the game had hurried on.

Now she had her back to a tree and was holding the lantern high. It glinted on his eyes. And the fourth time she shot, and something hot and strange singed by close to his head. But it wasn't the pain of one quill from a porcupine, and it only increased his anger. He waited, crouching, and the girl started on.

She was making other sounds now--queer, whimpering sounds not greatly different from the bleat that the fawn utters when it dies. It was a fear-sound, and if there is one emotion with which the wild beasts are acquainted, in all its phases, it is fear. She was afraid of him then, and that meant he need no longer be in the least afraid of her. His skin began to twitch all over with that terrible madness and passion of the flesh-hunters.

This game was like the deer, and the thing to do was lie in wait. There was only one trail. He was simply following his instincts, no conscious intelligence, when he made a long circle about her and turned back to the trail two hundred yards in front. He wasn't afraid of losing her in the darkness. She was neither fleet like the deer nor courageous like Woof, the bear. He had only to wait and leap from the darkness when she passed.

And because this was his own way of hunting, because the experiences of a thousand generations of cougars had taught him that it was the safest way, that even an elk may be downed by a surprise leap from ambush, the last of his fear went out of him. The step drew nearer, and he knew he would not again be afraid to give his stroke.

When Dan Failing, riding like mad over the mountain trail, heard the third shot from Snowbird's pistol, he felt that one of the debts he owed had come due at last. He seemed to know, as the darkness pressed around him, that he was to be tried in the fire. And the horse staggered beneath him as he tried to hasten.

He showed no mercy to his mount. Horseflesh isn't made for carrying a heavy man over such a trail as this, and she was red-nostriled and lathered before half a mile had been covered. He made her leap up the rocks, and on the fairly level stretches he loosed the reins and lashed her into a gallop. Only a mountain horse could have stood that test. To Dan's eyes, the darkness was absolute; yet she kept straight to the trail. He made no attempt to guide her.

She bounded over logs that he couldn't see, and followed turn after turn in the trail without ever a misstep.

He gave no thought to his own safety. His courage was at the test, and no risk of his own life must interfere with his attempt to save Snowbird from the danger that threatened her. He didn't know when the horse would fall with him and precipitate him down a precipice, and he was perfectly aware that to crash into a low-hanging limb of one of the great trees beside the trail would probably crush his skull. But he took the chance. And before the ride was done he found himself pleading with the horse, even as he lashed her sides with his whip.

The lesser forest creatures sprang from his trail; and once the mare leaped high to miss a dark shadow that crossed in front. As she caught her stride, Dan hear(i a squeal and a rattle of quills that identified the creature as a porcupine.

By now he had passed the first of the worst grades, coming out upon a long, easy slope of open forest. Again he urged his horse, leaving to her keen senses alone the choosing of the path between the great tree trunks. He rode almost in silence. The deep carpet of pine needles, wet from the recent rains, dulled the sound of the horse's hoofs.

Then he heard Snowbird fire for the fourth time; and he knew that he had almost overtaken her. The report seemed to smash the air. And he lashed his horse into the fastest run she knew,--a wild, sobbing figure in the darkness.

"She's only got one shot more," he said. He knew how many bullets her pistol carried; and the danger--whatever it was--must be just at hand. Underbrush cracked beneath him. And then the horse drew up with a jerk that almost hurled him from the saddle.

He lashed at her in vain. She was not afraid of the darkness and the rocks of the trail, but some Terror in the woods in front had in an instant broken his control over her. She reared, snorting; then danced in an impotent circle. Meanwhile, precious seconds were fleeing.

He understood now. The horse stood still, shivering beneath him, but would not advance a step. The silence deepened. Somewhere in the darkness before him a great cougar was waiting by the trail, and Snowbird, hoping for the moment that it had given up the chase, was hastening through the shadows squarely into its ambush.

Whisperfoot crouched lower: and again his long serpent of a tail began the little vertical motion that always precedes his leap. He had not forgotten the wild rapture of that moment he had inadvertently sprung on Landy Hildreth,-- or how, after his terror had died, he had come creeping back. He hunted his own way, waiting on the trail; and his madness was at its height. He was not just Whisperfoot the coward, that runs at the shadow of a tall form in the thickets. The consummation was complete, and that single experience of a month before had made of him a hunter of men. His muscles set for the leap.

So intent was he that his keen senses didn't detect the fact that there was a curious echo to the girl's footsteps. Dan Failing had slipped down from his terrified horse and was running up the trail behind her, praying that he could be in time.

Snowbird heard the pat, pat of his feet; but at first she did not dare to hope that aid had come to her. She had thought of Dan as on the far-away marshes; and her father, the only other living occupant of this part of the Divide, might even now be lying dead in his house. In her terror, she had lost all power of interpretation of events. The sound might be the cougar's mate, or even the wolf pack, jealous of his game. Sobbing, she hurried on into Whisperfoot's ambush.

Then she heard a voice, and it seemed to be calling to her. "Snowbird--I'm coming, Snowbird," a man's strong voice was shouting. She whirled with a sob of thankfulness.

At that instant the cougar sprang.

Terrified though she was, Snowbird's reflexes had kept sure and true. Even as the great cat leaped, a long, lithe shadow out of the shadow, her finger pressed back against the trigger of her pistol. She had been carrying her gun in front of her, and she fired it, this last time, with no conscious effort. It was just a last instinctive effort to defend herself.

One other element affected the issue. She had whirled to answer Dan's cry just as the cougar left the ground. But she had still been in range. The only effect was to lessen, in some degree, the accuracy of the spring. The bullet caught the beast in mid-air; but even if it had reached its heart, the momentum of the attack was too great to be completely overcome. Snowbird only knew that some vast, resistless power had struck her, and that the darkness seemed to roar and explode about her.

Hurled to her face in the trail, she did not see the cougar sprawl on the earth beside her. The flame in the lantern almost flicked out as it fell from her hand, then flashed up and down, from the deepest gloom to a vivid glare with something of the effect of lightning flickering in the sky. Nor did she hear the first frenzied thrashing of the wounded animal. Kindly unconsciousness had fallen, obscuring this and also the sight of the great cat, in the agony of its wound, creeping with broken shoulder and bared claws across the pine needles toward her defenseless body.

But the terrible fangs were never to know her white flesh. Some one had come between. There was no chance to shoot: Whisperfoot and the girl were too near together for that. But one course remained; and there was not even time to count the cost. In this most terrible moment of Dan Failing's life, there was not even an instant's hesitation. He did not know that Whisperfoot was wounded. He saw the beast creeping forward in the weird dancing light of the fallen lantern, and he only knew that his flesh, not hers, must resist its rending talons. Nothing else mattered. No other considerations could come between.

It was the test; and Dan's instincts prompted coolly and well. He leaped with all his strength. The cougar bounded into his arms, not upon the prone body of the girl. And she opened her eyes to hear a curious thrashing in the pine needles, a strange grim battle that, as the lantern flashed out, was hidden in the darkness.

And that battle, in the far reaches of the Divide, passed into a legend. It was the tale of how Dan Failing, his gun knocked from his hands as he met the cougar's leap, with his own unaided arms kept the life-giving breath from the animal's lungs and killed him in the pine needles. Claw and fang and the frenzy of death could not matter at all.

Thus Failing established before all men his right to the name he bore. And thus he paid one of his debts--life for a life, as the code of the forest has always decreed--and in the fire of danger and pain his metal was tried and proven.

BOOK THREE

THE PAYMENT

The Lennox home, in the far wilderness of the Umpquaw Divide, looked rather like an emergency hospital for the first few days after Dan's fight with Whisperfoot. Its old sounds of laughter and talk were almost entirely lacking. Two injured men and a girl recovering from a nervous collapse do not tend toward cheer.

But the natural sturdiness of all three quickly came to their aid. Of course Lennox had been severely injured by the falling log, and many weeks would pass before he would be able to walk again. He could sit up for short periods, however; had the partial use of one arm; and could propel himself--after the first few weeks--at a snail's pace through the rooms in a rude wheel chair that Bill's ingenuity had contrived. The great livid scratches that Dan bore on his body quickly began to heal; and before a week was done, he began to venture forth on the hills again. Snowbird had remained in bed for three days: then she had hopped out, one bright afternoon, swearing never to go back into it again. Evidently the crisp 禄 fall air of the mountains had been a nerve tonic for them all.

Of course there had been medical attention. A doctor and a nurse had motored up the day after the accident; the physician had set the bones and departed, and the nurse remained for a week, to see the grizzled mountaineer well on the way of convalescence. But it was an anxious wait, and Lennox's car was kept constantly in readiness to speed her away in case the snows should start. At last she had left him in Snowbird's hands, and Bill had driven her back to the settlements in his father's car. The die was now cast as to whether or not Dan and the remainder of the family should winter in the mountains. The snow clouds deepened every day, the frost was ever heavier in the dawns, and the road would surely remain open only a few days more.

Once more the three seemingly had the Divide all to themselves. Bert Cranston had evidently deserted his cabin and was working a trap-line on the Umpquaw side. The rangers left the little station, all danger of fire past, and went down to their offices in the Federal building of one of the little cities below. Because he was worse than useless in the deep snows that were sure to come, one of the ranch hands that had driven up with Bill rode away to the valleys the last of the live stock,--the horse that Dan had ridden to Snowbird's defense.

Nothing had been heard of Landy Hildreth, who used to live on the trail to the marsh, and both Lennox and his daughter wondered why. There were also certain officials who had begun to be curious. As yet, Dan had told no one of the grim find he had made on his return from hunting. And he would have found it an extremely difficult fact to explain.

It all went back to those inner springs of motive that few men can see clearly enough within themselves to recognize. Even the first day, when he lay burning from his wounds, he worked out his own explanation in regard to the murder mystery. He hadn't the slightest doubt but that Cranston had killed Hildreth to prevent his testimony from reaching the courts below. Of course any other member of the arson ring of hillmen might have been the murderer; yet Dan was inclined to believe that Cranston, the leader of the gang, usually preferred to do such dangerous work as this himself. If it were true, somewhere on that tree-clad ridge clues would be left. By a law that went down to the roots of life, he knew, no action is so small but that it leaves its mark.

Moreover, it was wholly possible that the written testimony Hildreth must have gathered had never been found or destroyed. Dan didn't want the aid of the courts to find these clues. He wanted to work out the case himself. It resolved itself into a simple matter of vengeance: Dan had his debt to pay, and he wanted to bring Cranston to ruin by his own hand alone. While it was true that he took rather more than the casual interest that most citizens feel in the destruction of the forest by wanton fire, and had an actual sense of duty to do all that he could to stop the activities of the arson ring, his motives, stripped and bare, were really not utilitarian. He had no particular interest in Hildreth's case. He remembered him simply as one of Cranston's disreputable gang, a poacher and a fire bug himself. When all is said and done, it remained really a personal issue between Dan and Cranston, And personal issues are frowned upon by law and society. Civilization has toiled up from the darkness in a great measure to get away from them. But human nature remains distressingly the same, and Dan's desire to pay his debt was a distinctly human emotion. Sometime a breed will live upon the earth that can get clear away from personal vengeance--from that age-old code of the hills that demands a blow for a blow and a life for a life--but the time is not yet. And after all, by all the standards of men as men, not as read in idealistic philosophies, Dan's debt was entirely real. By the light held high by his ancestors, he could not turn his other cheek.

Just as soon as he was able, he went back to the scene of the murder. He didn't know when the snow would come to cover what evidence there was. It threatened every hour. Every wind promised it. The air was sharp and cold, and no drop of rain could fall through it without crystallizing into snow. The deer had all gone, and the burrowing people had sought their holes. The bees worked no more in the winter flowers. Of all the greater forest creatures, only the wolves and the bear remained,--the former because their fear of men would not permit them to go down to the lower hills, and the latter because of his knowledge that when food became scarce, he could always burrow in the snow. No bear goes into hibernation from choice. Wise old bachelor, he much prefers to keep just as late hours as he can--as long as the eating places in the berry thickets remain open. The cougars had all gone down with the deer, the migratory birds had departed, and even the squirrels were in hiding.

The scene didn't offer much in the way of dues. Of the body itself, only a white heap of bones remained; for many and terrible had been the agents at work upon them. The clothes, however, particularly the coat, were practically intact. Gripping himself, Dan thrust his fingers into its pockets, then into the pockets of the shirt and trousers. All papers that would in any way serve to identify the murdered man, or tell what his purpose had been in journeying down the trail the night of the murder had been removed. Only one explanation presented itself. Cranston had come before him, and searched the body himself.

Dan looked about for tracks, and he was considerably surprised to find the blurred, indistinct imprint of a shoe other than his own. He hadn't the least hope that the tracks themselves would offer a clue to a detective. They were too dim for that. The surprising fact was that since the murder had been committed immediately before the fall rains, the water had not completely washed them out. The only possibility remaining was that Cranston had returned to the body after the week's rainfall. The track had been dimmed by the lighter rains that had fallen since.

But yet it was entirely to be expected that the examination of the body would be an afterthought on Cranston's part. Possibly at first his only thought was to kill and, following the prompting that has sent so many murderers to the gallows, he had afterwards returned to the scene of the crime to destroy any clues he might have left and to search the body for any evidence against the arson ring.

Dan's next thought was to follow along the trail and find Cranston's ambush. Of course it would be in the direction of the settlement from the body, as the bullet had entered from the front. He found it hard to believe that Hildreth had fallen in the exact spot where the body lay. Men journeying at night keep to the trail, and the white heap itself was fully forty feet back from the trail in the thickets. Perhaps Cranston had dragged it there to hide it from the sight of any one who might pass along the lonely trail again; and it was a remote possibility that Whisperfoot, coming in the night, had tugged it into the thickets for dreadful purposes of his own. Likely the shot was fired when Hildreth was in an open place on the trail; and Dan searched for the ambush with this conclusion in mind. He walked back, looking for a thicket from which such a spot would be visible. Something over fifty yards down he found it; and he knew it by the empty brass rifle cartridge that lay half buried in the wet leaves.

The shell was of the same caliber as Cranston's hunting rifle. Dan's hand shook as he put it in his pocket.

Encouraged by this amazing find, he turned up the trail toward Hildreth's cabin. It might be possible, he thought, that Hildreth had left some of his testimony--perhaps such rudely scrawled letters as Cranston had written him-

-in some forgotten drawer in his hut. It was but a short walk for Dan's hardened legs, and he made it before mid-afternoon.

The search itself was wholly without result. But because he had time to think as he climbed the ridge, because as he strode along beneath that wintry sky he had a chance to consider every detail of the case, he was able to start out on a new tack when, just before simset, he returned to the body. This new train of thought had as its basis that Cranston's shot had not been deadly at once; that wounded, Hildreth had himself crawled into the thickets where Whisperfoot had found him. And that meant that he had to enlarge his search for such documents as Hildreth had carried to include all the territory between the trail and the location of the body.

It was possibly a distance of forty feet, and getting down on his hands and knees, Dan looked for any break in the shrubbery that would indicate the path that the wounded Hildreth had taken. And it was ten minutes well rewarded, as far as clearing up certain details of the crime. His senses had been trained and sharpened by his months in the wilderness, and he was able to back-track the wounded man from the skeleton clear to the clearing on the trail where he had first fallen. But as no clues presented themselves, he started to turn home.

He walked twelve feet, then turned back. Out of the corner of his eye it seemed to him that he had caught a flash of white, near the end of a great, dead log beside the path that the wounded Hildreth had taken. It was to the credit of his mountain training alone that his eye had been keen enough to detect it; that it had been so faithfully recorded on his consciousness; and that, knowing at last the importance of details, he had turned back. For a moment he searched in vain. Evidently a yellow leaf had deceived him. Once more he retraced his steps, trying to find the position from which his eye had caught the glimpse of white. Then he dived straight for the rotten end of the log.

Into a little hollow in the bark, on the underside of the log, some hand had thrust a small roll of papers. They were rain soaked now, and the ink had dimmed and blotted; but Dan realized their significance. They were the complete evidence that Hildreth had accumulated against the arson ring,-- letters that had passed back and forth between himself and Cranston, a threat of murder from the former if Hildreth turned State's evidence, and a signed statement of the arson activities of the ring by Hildreth himself. They were not only enough to break up the ring and send its members to prison; with the aid of the empty shell and other circumstantial evidence, they could in all probability convict Bert Cranston of murder.

For a long time he stood with the shadows of the pines lengthening about him, his gray eyes in curious shadow. For the moment a glimpse was given him into the deep wells of the human soul; and understanding came to him. Was there no balm for hatred even in the moment of death? Were men unable to forget the themes and motives of their lives, even when the shadows closed down upon them? Hildreth had known what hand had struck him down. And even on the frontier of death, his first thought was to hide his evidence where Cranston could not find it when he searched the body, but where later it might be found by the detectives that were sure to come. It was the old creed of a life for a life. He wanted his evidence to be preserved,--not that right should be wronged, but so that Cranston would be prosecuted and convicted and made to suffer. His hatred of Cranston that had made him turn State's evidence in the first place had been carried with him down into death.

As Dan stood wondering, he thought he heard a twig crack on the trail behind him, and he wondered what forest creature was still lingering on the ridges at the eve of the snows.

II

The snow began to fall in earnest at midnight,--great, white flakes that almost in an instant covered the leaves. It was the real beginning of winter, and all living creatures knew it. The wolf pack sang to it from the ridge,--a wild and plaintive song that made Bert Cranston, sleeping in a lean-to on the Umpquaw side of the Divide, swear and mutter in his sleep. But he didn't really waken until Jim Gibbs, one of his gang, returned from his secret mission.

They wasted no words. Bert flung aside the blankets, lighted a candle, and placed it out of the reach of the night wind. It cast queer shadows in the lean-to and found a curious reflection in the steel points of his eyes. His face looked swarthy and deep-lined in its light.

"Well?" he demanded. "What did you find?"

"Nothin'," Jim Gibbs answered gutturally. "If you ask me what I found out, I might have somethin' to answer."

"Then--" and Bert, after the manner of his kind, breathed an oath--" what did you find out?"

His tone, except for an added note of savagery, remained the same. Yet his heart was thumping a great deal louder than he liked to have it. He wasn't amused by his associate's play on words. Nor did he like the man's knowing tone and his air of importance. Realizing that the snows were at hand, he had sent Gibbs for a last search of the body, to find and recover the evidence that Hildreth had against him and which had not been revealed either on Hildreth's person or in his cabin. He had become increasingly apprehensive about those letters he had written Hildreth, and certain other documents that had been in his possession. He didn't understand why they hadn't turned up. And now the snows had started, and Jim Gibbs had returned empty-handed, but evidently not empty-minded.

"I've found out that the body's been uncovered--and men are already searchin' for clues. And moreover--I think they've found them." He paused, weighing the effect of his words. His eyes glittered with cunning. Rat that he was, he was wondering whether the time had arrived to leave the ship. He had no intention of continuing to give his services to a man with a rope-noose closing about him. And Cranston, knowing this fact, hated him as he hated the buzzard that would claim him in the end and tried to hide his apprehension.

"Go on. Blat it out," Cranston ordered. "Or else go away and let me sleep."

It was a bluff; but it worked. If Gibbs had gone without speaking, Cranston would have known no sleep that night. But the man became more fawning.

"I'm tellin' you, fast as I can," he went on, almost whining. "I went to the cabin, just as you said. But I didn't get a chance to search it--"

"Why not?" Cranston thundered. His voice reechoed among the snow-wet pines.

"I'll tell you why! Because some one else--evidently a cop--was already searchin' it. Both of us know there's nothin' there anyway. We've gone over it too many times. After a while he went away--but I didn't turn back yet. That wouldn't be Jim Gibbs. I shadowed him, just as you'd want me to. And he went straight back to the body."

"Yes?" Cranston had hard work containing his impatience. Again Gibbs' eyes were full of ominous speculations.

"He stopped at the body, and it was plain he'd been there before. He went crawling through the thickets, lookin' for clues. He done what you and me never thought to do--lookin' all the way between the trail and the body. He'd already found the brass shell you told me to get. At least, it wasn't there when I looked, after he'd gone. You should've thought of it before. But he found somethin' else a whole lot more important--a roll of papers that Hildreth had chucked into an old pine stump when he was dyin'. It was your fault, Cranston, for not gettin' them that night. You needn't've been afraid of any one hearin' the shot and catching you red-handed. This detective stood and read 'em on the trail. And you know--just as well as I do--what they were."

"Damn you, I went back the next morning, as soon as I could see. And the mountain lion had already been there. I went back lots of times since. And that shell ain't nothing--but all the time I supposed I put it in my pocket. You know how it is--a fellow throws his empty shell out by habit."

Gibbs' eyes grew more intent. What was this thing? Cranston's tone, instead of commanding, was almost pleading. But the leader caught himself at once.

"I don't see why I need to explain any of that to you. What I want to know is this: why you didn't shoot and get those papers away from him?"

For an instant their eyes battled. But Gibbs had never the strength of his leader. If he had, it would have been asserted long since. He sucked in his breath, and his gaze fell away. It rested on Cranston's rifle, that in some manner had been pulled up across his knees. And at once he was cowed. He was never so fast with a gun as Cranston.

"Blood on my hands, eh--same as on yours?" he mumbled, looking down. "What do you think I want, a rope around my neck? These hills are big, but the arm of the law has reached up before, and it might again. You might as well know first as last I'm not goin' to do any killings to cover up your murders."

"That comes of not going myself. You fool--if he gets that evidence down to the courts, you're broken the same as me."

"But I wouldn't get more 'n a year or so, at most--and that's a heap different from the gallows. I did aim at him--"

"But you just lacked the guts to pull the trigger!"

"I did, and I ain't ashamed of it. But besides--the snows are here now, and he won't be able to even get word down to the valleys in six months. If you want him killed so bad, do it yourself."

This was a thought indeed. On the other hand, another murder might not be necessary. Months would pass before the road would be opened, and in the meantime Cranston could have a thousand chances to steal back the accusing letters. Perhaps they would be guarded closely at first, but by the late winter months they would be an old story, and a single raid on the house might turn the trick. He didn't believe for an instant that the man Gibbs had seen a detective. He had kept too close watch over the roads for that.

"A tall chap, in outing clothes--dark-haired and clean-shaven?"

"Yes?"

"Wears a tan hat?"

"That's the man."

"I know him--and I wish you'd punctured him. Why, you could've taken those papers away from him and slapped his face, and he wouldn't have put up his arms. And now he'll hide 'em somewhere--afraid to carry 'em for fear he meets me. That's Failing--the tenderfoot that's been staying at Lennox's. He's a lounger."

"He didn't look like no lounger to me."

"But no matter about that--it's just as I thought. And I'll get 'em back--mark my little words."

In the meantime the best thing to do was to move at once to his winter trapping grounds,--a certain neglected region on the lower levels of the North Fork. If at any time within the next few weeks, Dan should attempt to carry word down to the settlements, he would be certain to pass within view of this camp. But he knew that the chance of Dan starting upon any such journey before the snow had melted was not one in a thousand. To be caught in the Divide in the winter means to be snowed in as completely as the Innuits of upper Greenland. No word could pass except by a man on snowshoes. Really there was no urgency about this matter of the evidence.

Yet if the chance did come, if the house should be left unguarded, it might pay Cranston to make an immediate search. Dan would have no reason for supposing that Cranston suspected his possession of the letters; he would not be particularly watchful, and would probably pigeonhole them until spring in Lennox's desk.

And the truth was that Cranston had reasoned out the situation almost perfectly. When Dan wakened in the morning, and the snow lay already a foot deep over the wilderness world, he knew that he would have no chance to act upon the Cranston case until the snows melted in the spring. So he pushed all thought of it out of his mind and turned his attention to more pleasant subjects. It was true that he read the documents over twice as he lay in bed. Then he tied them into a neat packet and put them away where they would be quickly available. Then he thrust his head out of the window and let the great snowflakes sift down upon his face. It was winter at last, the season that he loved.

He didn't stir from the house, that first day of the storm. Snowbird and he found plenty of pleasant things to do and talk about before the roaring fire that he built in the grate. He was glad of the great pile of wood that lay outside the door. It meant life itself, in this season. Then Snowbird led him to the windows, and they watched the white drifts pile up over the low underbrush.

When finally the snowstorm ceased, five days later, the whole face of the wilderness was changed. The buckbrush was mostly covered, the fences were out of sight; the forest seemed a clear, clean sweep of white, broken only by an occasional tall thicket and by the great, snow-covered trees.

When the clouds blew away, and the air grew clear, the temperature began to fall. Dan had no way of knowing how low it went. Thermometers were not considered essential at the Lennox home. But when his eyelids congealed with the frost, and his mittens froze to the logs of firewood that he carried through the door, and the pine trees exploded and cracked in the darkness, he was correct in his belief that it Was very, very cold.

But he loved the cold, and the silence and austerity that went with it. The wilderness claimed him as never before. The rugged breed that were his ancestors had struggled through such seasons as this and passed a love of them down through the years to him.

When the ice made a crust over the snow, he learned to walk on snowshoes. At first there were pained ankles and endless floundering in the drifts. But between the fall of fresh snow and the thaws that softened the crust, he slowly mastered the art. Snowbird--and Dan never realized the full significance of her name until he saw her flying with incredible grace over the snow--laughed at him at first and ran him races that would usually end in his falling headfirst into a ten-foot snowbank. She taught him how to ski and more than once she would stop in the middle of an earnest bit of pedagogy to find that he wasn't listening at all. He would seem to be fairly devouring her with his eyes, delighting in the play of soft pinks and reds in her cheeks, and drinking, as a man drinks wine, the amazing change of light and shadow in her eyes.

She seemed to blossom under his gaze. Not one of those short winter days went by without the discovery of some new trait or little vanity to astonish or delight him,--sometimes an unlooked-for tenderness toward the weak, often a sweet, untainted philosophy of life, or perhaps just a lowering of her eyelids in which her eyes would show lustrous through the lashes, or some sweeping, exuberant gesture startlingly graceful.

Lennox wakened one morning with the realization that this was one of the hardest winters of his experience. More snow had fallen in the night and had banked halfway up his windows. The last of the shrubbery--except for the ends of a few tall bushes that would not hold the snow--was covered, and the roofs of some of the lower outbuildings had somewhat the impression of drowning things, striving desperately to keep their heads above water. He began to be very glad of the abundant stores of provisions that overcrowded his pantry--savory hams and bacons, dried venison, sacks of potatoes and evaporated vegetables, and, of course, canned goods past counting. With the high fire roaring in the grate, the season held no ills for them. But sometimes^ when the bitter cold came down at twilight, and the moon looked like a thing of ice itself over the snow, he began to wonder how the wild creatures who wintered on the Divide were faring. Of course most of them were gone. Woof, long since, had grunted and mumbled his way into a winter lair. But the wolves remained, strange gray-shadows on the snow, and possibly a few of the hardier smaller creatures.

More than once in those long winter nights their talk was chopped off short by the song of the pack on some distant ridge. Sometime, when the world is old, possibly a man will be born that can continue to talk and keep his mind on his words while the wolf pack sings. But he is certainly an unknown quantity today. The cry sets in vibration curious memory chords, and for a moment the listener sees in his mind's eye his ancient home in an ancient world,--Darkness and Fear and Eyes shining about the cave. It carries him back, and he knows the wilderness as it really is; and to have such knowledge dries up all inclination to talk, as a sponge dries water. Of course the picture isn't entirely plain. It is more a thing guessed at, a photograph in some dark part of an under-consciousness that has constantly grown more dim as the centuries have passed. Possibly sometime it will fade out altogether; and then a man may continue to discuss the weather while the Song from the ridge shudders in at the windows. But the world will be quite cold by then, and no longer particularly interesting. And possibly even the wolves themselves will then be tamed to play dead and speak pieces,--which means the wilderness itself will be tamed. For as long as the wild lasts, the pack will run through it in the winter. They were here in the beginning, and in spite of constant war and constant hatred on the part of men, they will be here in the end. The reason is just that they are the symbol of the wilderness itself, and the idea of it continuing to exist without them is stranger than that of a nation without a flag.

It wasn't quite the same song that Dan had listened to in the first days of fall. It had been triumphant then, and proud with the wilderness pride. Of course it had been sad then, too, but it was more sad now. And it was stranger, too, and crept farther into the souls of its listeners. It was the song of strength that couldn't avail 悖 gainst the snow, possibly of cold and the despair and courage of starvation. These three that heard it were inured to the wilderness; but a moment was always needed after its last note had died to regain their gayety.

"They're getting lean and they're getting savage," Lennox said one night, stretched on his divan before the fireplace. He was still unable to walk; but the fractures were knitting slowly and the doctor had promised that the summer would find him well. "If we had a dog, I wouldn't offer much for his life. One of these days we'll find 'em in a big circle around the house--and then we'll have to open up with the rifles."

But this picture appalled neither of his two young listeners. No wolf pack can stand against three marksmen, armed with rifles and behind oaken walls.

Christmas came and passed, and January brought clear days and an ineffective sun shining on the snow. These were the best days of all. Every afternoon Dan and Snowbird would go out on their skis or on snowshoes, unarmed except for the pistol that Snowbird carried in the deep pocket of her mackinaw. "But why not?" Dan replied to Lennox's objection. "She could kill five wolves with five shots, or pretty near it, and you know well enough that that would hold 'em off till we got home. They'd stop to eat the five. I have hard enough time keeping up with her as it is, without carrying a rifle." And Lennox was content. In the first place 禄 the wolf pack has to he desperate indeed before it will even threaten human beings; and knowing the coward that the wolf is in the other three seasons, he couldn't bring himself to believe that this point was reached. In the second, Dan had told the truth when he said that five deaths, or even fewer, would repel the attack of any wolf pack he had ever seen. There was just one troubling thought. He had heard, long ago, and he had forgotten who had told him, that in the most severe winters the wolves gather in particularly large packs; and a quality in the song that they had heard at night seemed to bear it out. The chorus had been exceptionally loud and strong, and he had been unable to pick out individual voices.

The snow was perfect for skiing. Previously their sport had been many times interrupted either by the fall of fresh snow or a thaw that had softened the snow crust; but now every afternoon was too perfect to remain indoors. They shouted and romped in the silences, and they did not dream but that they had the wilderness all to themselves. The fact that one night Lennox's keen eyes had seen what looked like the glow of a camp fire in the distance didn't affect this belief of theirs at all.

It was evidently just the phosphorus glowing in a rotten log from which the winds had blown the snow.

Once or twice they caught glimpses of wild life: once a grouse that had buried in the snow flushed from their path and blew the snow-dust from its wings; and once or twice they saw snowshoe rabbits bounding away on flat feet over the drifts. But just one day they caught sight of a wolf. They were on snowshoes on a particularly brilliant afternoon late in January.

He was a lone male, evidently a straggler from the pack, and he leaped from the top of a tall thicket that had remained above the snow. The man and the girl had entirely different reactions. Dan's first impression was amazement at the animal's condition. It seemed to be in the last stages of starvation: unbelievably gaunt, with rib bones showing plainly even through the furry hide. Ordinarily the heavily furred animals do not show signs of famine; but even an inexperienced eye could not make a mistake in this case. The eyes were red, and they carried Dan back to his first adventure in the Oregon forest--the day he had shot the mad coyote. Snowbird thought of the beast only as an enemy. The wolves killed her father's stock; they were brigands of the worst order; and she shared the hatred of them that is a common trait of all primitive peoples. Her hand whipped back, seized her pistol, and she fired twice at the fleeing figure.

The second shot was a hit: both of them saw the wolf go to its side, then spring up and race on. Shouting, both of them sped after him.

In a few moments he was out of sight among the distant trees, but they found the blood-trail and mushed over the ridge. They expected at any moment to find him lying dead; but the track led them on clear down the next canyon. And now they cared not at all whether they found him: it was simply a tramp in the out-of-doors; and both of them were young with red. blood in their veins.

But all at once Dan stopped in his tracks. The girl sped on for six paces before she missed the sound of his snowshoes; then she turned to find him standing, wholly motionless, with eyes fixed upon her.

It startled her, and she didn't know why. A companion abruptly freezing in his path, his muscles inert, and his eyes filling with speculations is always startling. When this occurs, it means simply that a thought so compelling and engrossing that even the half-unconscious physical functions, such as walking, cannot continue, has come into his mind. And it is part of the old creed of self-preservation to dislike greatly to be left out on any such thought as this. If danger is present, the sooner it is identified the better.

"What is it?" she demanded.

He turned to her, curiously intent. "How many shells have you in that pistol?"

She took one breath and answered him. "It holds five, and I shot twice. I haven't any others."

"And I don't suppose it ever occurred to you to carry extra ones in your pocket?"

"Father is always telling me to--and several times I have. But I'd shoot them away at target practice and forget to take any more. There was never any danger--except that night with a cougar. I did intend to--but what does it matter now?"

"We're a couple of wise ones, going after that wolf with only three shots to our name. Of course by himself he's harmless--but he's likely enough to lead us straight toward the pack. And Snowbird--I didn't like his looks. He's too gaunt, and he's too hungry--and I haven't a bit of doubt he waited in that brush for us to come, intending to attack us--and lost his nerve the last thing. That shows he's desperate. I don't like him, and I wouldn't like his pack. And a whole pack might not lose its nerve."

"Then you think we'd better turn back?" "Yes, I do, and not come out any more without a whole pocket of shells. I'm going to carry my rifle, too, just as Lennox has always advised. He's only got a flesh-wound. You saw what you did with two cartridges

--got in one flesh-wound. Three of 'em against a pack wouldn't be a great deal of aid. I don't mean to say you can't shoot, but a jumping, lively wolf is worse than a bu-d in the air. We've gone over three miles; and he'd lead us ten miles farther--even if he didn't go to the pack. Let's go back."

"If you say so. But I don't think there's the least bit of danger. We can always climb a tree."

"And have 'em make a beautiful circle under it! They've got more patience than we have

--and we'd have to come down sometime. Your father can't come to our help, you know. It's the sign of the tenderfoot not to think there's any danger--and I'm not going to think that way any more."

They turned back and mushed in silence a long time.

"I suppose you'll think I'm a coward," Dan asked her humbly.

"Only prudent, Dan," she answered, smiling. Whether she meant it, he did not know. "I'm just beginning to understand that you--living here only a few months--really know and understand all this better than I do." She stretched her arms wide to the wilderness. "I guess it's your instincts."

"And I do understand," he told her earnestly. "I sensed danger back there just as sure as I can see your face. That pack--and it's a big one--is close; and it's terribly hungry. And you know--you can't help but know--that the wolves are not to be trusted in famine times."

"I know it only too well," she said.

Then she paused and asked him about a strange grayness, like snow blown by the wind, on the sky over the ridge.

III

Bebt Cranston waited in a clump of exposed thicket on the hillside until he saw two black dots, that he knew were Dan and Snowbird, leave the Lennox home. He lay very still as they circled up the ridge, noticing that except for the pistol that he knew Snowbird always carried, they were unarmed. There was no particular reason why he should be interested in that point. It was just the mountain way always to look for weapons, and it is rather difficult to trace the mental processes behind this impulse. Perhaps it can be laid to the fact that many mountain families are often at feud with one another, and anything in the way of violence may happen before the morning.

The two passed out of his sight, and after a long time he heard the crack of Snowbird's pistol. He guessed that she had either shot at some wild creature, or else was merely at target practice,--rather a common proceeding for the two when they were on the hills together. Thus it is to be seen that Cranston knew their habits fairly well. And since he had kept a close watch upon them for several days, this was to be expected.

He had no intention of being interrupted in this work he was about to do. He had planned it all very well. At first the intermittent snowstorms and the thaws between had delayed him. He needed a perfect snow crust for the long tramp over the ridge; and at last the bright days and the icy dawns had made it. The elder Lennox was still helpless. He had noticed that when Dan and Snowbird went out, they were usually gone from two to four hours; and that gave him plenty of time for his undertaking. The moment had come at last to make a thorough search of Lennox's house for those incriminating documents that Dan had found near the body of Landy Hildreth.

The only really dangerous, part of his undertaking was his approach. If by any chance Lennox were looking out of the window, he might be ffound waiting with a rifle across his arms. It would be quite like the old mountaineer to have his gun beside him, and to shoot it quick and exceptionally straight, without asking questions, at any stealing figure in the snow. Yet Cranston felt fairly sure that Lennox was still too helpless to raise a gun to a shooting position.

He had observed that the mountaineer spent his time either on the fireplace divan or on his own bed. Neither of these places was available to the rear windows of the house. So, very wisely, he made his attack from the rear.

He came stealing across the snow,--a musher of the first degree. Very silently and swiftly he slipped off his snowshoes at the door. The doQr itself was unlocked, just as he had supposed. In an instant more he was tiptoeing, a dark, silent figure, through the corridors of the house. He held his rifle ready in his hands.

He peered into Lennox's bedroom first. The room was unoccupied. Then the floor of the corridor creaked beneath his step; and he knew nothing further was to be gained by waiting. If Lennox suspected his presence, he might be waiting with aimed rifle as he opened the door of the living room.

He glided faster. He halted once more,--a moment at the living-room door to see if Lennox had been disturbed. He was lying still, however, so Cranston pushed through.

Lennox glanced up from his magazine to find that unmistakable thing, the barrel of a rifle, pointed at his breast. Cranston was one of those rare marksmen who shoots with both eyes open,--and that meant that he kept his full visual powers to the last instant before the hammer fell.

"I can't raise my arms," Lennox said simply. "One of 'em won't work at all-- besides, against the doctor's orders."

Cranston stole over toward him, looking closely for weapons. He pulled aside the woolen blanket that Lennox had drawn up over his body, and he pushed his hand into the cushions of the couch. A few deft pats, holding his rifle through the fork of his arm, finger coiled into the trigger guard, assured him that Lennox was not "heeled" at all. Then he laughed and went to work.

"I thought I told you once," Lennox began with perfect coldness, "that the doors of my house were no longer open to you." .

"You did say that," was Cranston's guttural reply. "But you see I'm here just the same, don't you? And what are you going to do about it?"

"I probably felt that sooner or later you would come to steal--just as you and your crowd stole the supplies from the forest station last winter--and that probably influenced me to give the orders. I didn't want thieves around my house, and I don't want them now, I don't want coyotes, either."

"And I don't want any such remarks out of you, either," Cranston answered him. "You lie still and shut up, and I suspect that sissy boarder of yours will come back, after he's through embracing your daughter in the snow, and find you in one piece. Otherwise not."

"If I were in one piece," Lennox answered him very quietly, "instead of a bundle of broken bones that can't lift its arms, I'd get up off this couch, unarmed as I am, and stamp on your lying lips."

But Cranston only laughed and tied Lennox's feet with a cord from the window shade.

He went to work very systematically. First he rifled Lennox's desk in the living room. Then he looked on all the mantels and ransacked the cupboards and the drawers. He was taunting and calm at first. But as the moments passed, his passion grew upon him. He no longer smiled. The rodent features became intent; the eyes narrowed to curious, bright lights under the dark lashes. He went to Dan's room, searched his bureau drawer and all the pockets of the clothes hanging in his closet. He upset his trunk and pawed among old letters in the suitcase. Then, stealing like some creature of the wilderness, he came back to the living room.

Lennox was not on the divan where he had left him. He lay instead on the floor near the fireplace; and he met the passion-drawn face with entire calmness. His motives were perfectly plain. He had just made a desperate effort to procure Dan's rifle that hung on two sets of deer horns over the fireplace, and was entirely exhausted from it. He had succeeded in getting down from the couch, though wracked by agony, but had been unable to lift himself up in reach of the gun.

Cranston read his intention in one glance. Lennox knew it, but he simply didn't care. He had passed the point where anything seemed to matter.

"Tell me where it is," Cranston ordered him. Again he pointed his rifle at Lennox's wasted breast.

"Tell you where what is? My money?"

"You know what I want--and it isn't money. I mean those letters that Failing found on the ridge. I'm through fooling, Lennox. Dan learned that long ago, and it's time you learned it now."

"Dan learned it because he was sick. He isn't sick now. Don't presume too much on that."

Cranston laughed with harsh scorn. "But that isn't the question. I said I've wasted all the time I'm going to. You are an old man and helpless; but I'm not going to let that stand in the way of getting what I came to get. They're hidden somewhere around this house. They wouldn't be out in the snow, because he'd want 'em where he could get them. By no means would he carry them on his person--fearing that some day he'd meet me on the ridge. He's a fool, but he ain't that much of a fool. I've watched, and he's had no chance to take them into town. I'll give you--just five seconds to tell me where they're hidden."

"And I give you," Lennox replied, "one second less than that--to go to Hell!"

Both of them breathed hard in the quiet room. Cranston was trembling now, shivering just a little in his arms and shoulders. "Don't get me wrong, Lennox," he warned.

"And don't have any delusions in regard to me, either," Lennox replied. "I've stood worse pain, from this accident, than any man can give me while I yet live, no matter what he does. If you want to get on me and hammer me in the approved Cranston way, I can't defend myself--but you won't get a civil answer out of me. I'm used to pain, and I can stand it. I'm not used to fawning to a coyote like you, and I can't stand it."

But Cranston hardly heard. An idea had flamed in his mind and cast a red glamour over all the scene about him. It was instilling a poison in his nerves and a madness in his blood, and it was searing him, like fire, in his dark brain. Nothing seemed real. He suddenly bent forward, tense.

"That's all right about you," he said. "But you'd be a little more polite if it was Snowbird--and Dan--that would have to pay."

Perhaps the color faded slightly in Lennox's face; but his voice did not change.

"They'll see your footprints before they come in and be ready," Lennox replied evenly. "They always come by the back way. And even with a pistol, Snowbird's a match for you."

"Did you think that was what I meant?" Cranston scorned. "I know a way to destroy those letters, and I'll do it--in the four seconds that I said, unless you tell. I'm not even sure I'm goin' to give you a chance to tell now; it's too good a scheme. There won't be any witnesses then to yell around in the courts. What if I choose to set fire to this house?"

"It wouldn't surprise me a great deal. It's your own trade." Lennox shuddered once on his place on the floor.

"I wouldn't have to worry about those letters then, would I? They are somewhere in the house, and they'd be burned to ashes. But that isn't all that would be burned. You could maybe crawl out, but you couldn't carry the guns, and you couldn't carry the pantry full of food. You're nearly eighty miles up here from the nearest occupied house, with two pair of snowshoes for the three of you and one dinky pistol. And you can't walk at all. It would be a nice pickle, wouldn't it? Wouldn't you have a fat chance of getting down to civilization?"

The voice no longer held steady. It trembled with passion. This was no idle threat. The brain had already seized upon the scheme with every intention of carrying it out. Outside the snow glittered in the sunlight, and pine limbs bowed with their load; overhung with that curious winter silence that, once felt, returns often in dreams. The wilderness lay stark and bare, stripped of all delusion--not only in the snow world outside but in the hearts of these two men, its sons.

"I have only one hope," Lennox replied. "I hope, unknown to me, that Dan has already dispatched those letters. The arm of the law is long, Cranston. It's easy to forget I that fact up here. It will reach you in the I end."

Cranston turned through the door, into the kitchen. He was gone a long time. Lennox heard him at work: the crinkle of paper and then a pouring sound around the walls. Then he heard the sharp crack of a match. An instant later the first wisp of smoke came curling, pungent with burning oil, through the corridor.

"You crawled from your couch to reach that gun," Cranston told him when he came in. "Let's see you crawl out now."

Lennox's answer was a curse,--the last, dread outpouring of an unbroken will. He didn't look again at the glittering eyes. He scarcely watched Cranston's further preparations: the oil poured on the rugs and furnishings, the kindling placed at the base of the curtains. Cranston was trained in this work. He was taking no chances on the fire being extinguished. And Lennox began to crawl toward the door.

He managed to grasp the corner of the blanket on the divan as he went, and he dragged it behind him. Pain wracked him, and smoke half-blinded him. But he made it at last. And by the time he had crawled one hundred feet over the snow crust, the whole structure was in flames. The red tongues spoke with a roar.

Cranston, the fire-madness on his face, hurried to the outbuildings. There he repeated the work. He touched a match to the hay in the bam, and the wind flung the flame through it in an instant. The sheds and other outbuildings were treated with oil. And seeing that his work was done, he called once to the prone body of Lennox on the snow and mushed away into the silences.

Lennox's answer was not a curse this time. Rather it was a prayer, unuttered, and in his long years Lennox had not prayed often. When he prayed at all, the words were burning fire. His prayer was that of Samson,--that for a moment his strength might come back to him.

IV

Two miles across the ridges, Dan and Snowbird saw a faint mist blowing between the trees. They didn't recognize it at first. It might be fine snow, blown by the wind, or even one of those mysterious fogs that sometimes sweep over the snow.

But it looks like smoke," Snowbird said. But it couldn't be. The trees are too wet to burn."

But then a sound that at first was just the faintest whisper in which neither of them would let themselves believe, became distinct past all denying. It was that menacing crackle of a great fire, that in the whole world of sounds is perhaps the most terrible. They were trained by the hills, and neither of them tried to mince words. They had learned to face the truth, and they faced it now.

"It's our house," Snowbird told him. "And father can't get out."

She spoke very quietly. Perhaps the most terrible truths of life are always spoken in that same quiet voice. Then both of them started across the snow, fast as their unwieldy snowshoes would permit.

"He can crawl a little," Dan called to her. "Don't give up, Snowbird mine. I think he'll be safe."

They mounted to the top of the ridge; and the long sweep of the forest was revealed to them. The house was a singular tall pillar of flame, already glowing that dreadful red from which firemen, despairing, turn away. Then the girl seized his hands and danced about him in a mad circle.

"He's alive," she cried. "You can see him--just a dot on the snow. He crawled out to safety."

She turned and sped at a breakneck pace down the ridge. Dan had to race to keep up with her. But it wasn't entirely wise to try to mush so fast. A dead log lay beneath the snow with a broken limb stretched almost to its surface, and it caught her snowshoe. The wood cracked sharply, and she fell forward in the snow. But she wasn't hurt, and the snowshoe itself, in spite of a small crack in the wood, was still serviceable.

"Haste makes waste," he told her. "Keep your feet on the ground, Snowbird; the house is gone already and your father is safe. Remember what lies before us."

The thought sobered and halted her. She glanced once at the dark face of her companion. Dan couldn't understand the strange light that suddenly leaped to her eyes. Perhaps she herself couldn't have explained the wave of tenderness that swept over her,--with no cause except the look in Dan's earnest gray eyes and the lines that cut so deep. Since the world was new, it has been the boast of the boldest of men that they looked their Fate in the face. And this is no mean looking. For fate is a sword from the darkness, a power that reaches out of the mystery, and cannot be classed with sights of human origin. It biuns out the eyes of all but the strongest men. Yet Dan was looking at his fate now, and his eyes held straight.

They walked together down to the ruined house, and the three of them sat silent while the fire burned red. Then Lennox turned to them with a half-smile.

"You're wasting time, you two," he said. "Remember all our food is gone. If you start now, and walk hard, maybe you can make it out."

"There are several things to do first," Dan answered simply.

"I don't know what they are. It isn't go-ing to be any picnic, Dan. A man can travel only so far without food to keep up his strength, particularly over sfuch ridges as you have to cross. It will be easy to give up and die. It's the test, man;

it's the test."

"And what about you?" his daughter asked.

"Oh, I'll be all right. Besides--it's the only thing that can be done. I can't walk, and you can't carry me on your backs. What else remains? I'll stay here--and I'll scrape together enough wood to keep a fire. Then you can bring help."

He kept his eyes averted when he talked. He was afraid for Dan to see them, knowing that he could read the lie in them.

"How do you expect to find wood--in this snow?" Dan asked him. "It will take four days to get out; do you think you could lie here and battle with a fire for four days, and then four days more that it will take to come back? You'd have two choices: to burn green wood that I'd cut for you before I left, or the rain-soaked dead wood under the snow. You couldn't keep either one of them burning, and you'd die in a night. Besides--this is no time for an unarmed man to be alone in the hills."

Lennox's voice grew pleading. "Be sensible, Dan!" he cried. "That Cranston's got us, and got us right. I've only one thing more I care about--and that is that you pay the debt! I can't hope to get out myself. I say that I can't even hope to. But if you bring my daughter through--and when the spring comes, pay what we owe to Cranston--I'll be content. Heavens, son--I've lived my life. The old pack leader dies when his time comes, and so does a man."

His daughter crept to him and sheltered his gray head against her breast. "I'll stay with you then," she cried.

"Don't be a little fool, Snowbird," he urged. "My clothes are wet already from the melted snow. It's too long a way--it will be too hard a fight, and children--I'm old and tired out. I don't want to make the try--hunger and cold; and even if you'd stay here and grub wood, Snowbird, they'd find us both dead when they came back in a week. We can't live without food, and work and keep warm--and there isn't a living creature in the hills."

"Except the wolves," Dan reminded him.

"Except the wolves," Lennox echoed. "Remember, we're unarmed--and they'd find it out. You're young, Snowbird, and so is Dan--and you two will be happy. I know how things are, you two--more than you know yourselves--and in the end you'll be happy. But me--I'm too tired to make the try. I don't care about it enough. I'm going to wave you good-by, and smile, and lie here and let the cold come down. You feel warm in a little while--"

But she stopped his lips with her hand. And he bent and kissed it.

"If anybody's going to stay with you," Dan told them in a clear, firm voice, "it's going to be me. But aren't any of the cabins occupied?"

"You know they aren't," Lennox answered. "Not even the houses beyond the North Fork, even if we could get across. The nearest help is over seventy miles."

"And Snowbird, think! Haven't any supplies been left in the ranger station?"

"Not one thing," the girl told him. "You know Cranston and his crowd robbed the place last winter. And the telephone lines were disconnected when the rangers left."

"Then the only way is for me to stay here. You can take the pistol, and you'll have a fair chance of getting through. I'll grub wood for our camp meanwhile, and you can bring help."

"And if the wolves come, or if help didn't come in time," Lennox whispered, passion-drawn for the first time, "who would pay what we owe to Cranston?"

"But her life counts--first of all."

"I know it does--but mine doesn't count at all. Believe me, you two. I'm speaking from my own desires when I say I don't want to make the fight. Snowbird would never make it through alone. There are the wolves, and maybe Cranston too--the worst woK of all. A woman can't mush across those ridges four days without food, without some one who loves her and forces her on! Neither can she stay here with me and try to make green branches burn in a fire. She's got three little pistol balls--and we'd all die for a whim. Oh, please, please--"

But Dan leaped for his hand with glowing eyes. "Listen, man! "he cried. "I know another way yet. I know more than one way; but one, if we've got the strength, is almost sure. There is an ax in the kitchen, and the blade will still be good."

"Likely dulled with the fire--" "I'll cut a limb with my jackknife for the handle. There will be nails in the ashes, plenty of them. We'll make a rude sledge, and we'll get you out too."

Lennox seemed to be studying his wasted hands. "It's a chance, but it isn't worth it," he said at last. "You'll have fight enough, without tugging at a heavy sled. It will take all night to build it, and it would cut down your chances of getting out by pretty near half. Remember the ridges, Dan--"

"But we'll climb every ridge--besides, its a slow, down grade most of the way, Snowbird--tell him he must do it."

Snowbird told him, overpowering him with her enthusiasm. And Dan shook his shoulders with rough hands. "You're hurting, boy!"

Lennox warned. "I'm a bag of broken bones."

"I'll tote you down there if I have to tie you in," Dan Failing replied. "Before, I've bowed to your will; but this time you have to bow to mine. I'm not going to let you stay here and die, no matter if you beg on your knees! It's the test-- and I'm going to bring you through."

He meant what he said. If mortal strength and sinew could survive such a test, he would succeed. There was nothing in these words to suggest the physical weakling that both of them had known a few months before. The eyes were earnest, the dark face intent, the determined voice did not waver at all.

"Dan Failing speaks!" Lennox replied with glowing eyes. He was recalling another Dan Failing of the dead years, a boyhood hero, and his remembered voice had never been more determined, more masterful than this he had just heard.

"And Cranston didn't get his purpose, after all." To prove his words, Dan thrust his hand into his inner coat pocket. He drew forth a little, flat package, haK as thick as a pack of cards. He held it up for them to see. "The thing Bert Cranston burned the house down to destroy," he explained. "I'm learning to know this mountain breed, Lennox. I kept it in my pocket where I could fight for it, at any minute."

Cranston had been mistaken, after all, in thinking that in fear of himself Dan would be afraid to keep the packet on his person, and would eventually conceal it in the house. He would have been even more surprised to know that Dan had lived in constant hope of meeting Cranston on the ridges, showing him what it contained, and fighting him for it, hands to hands. And even yet, perhaps the day would come when Cranston would know at last that Snowbird's words, after the fight of long ago, were true.

The twilight was falling over the snow, so Snowbird and Dan turned to the toil of building a sled.

The snow was steel-gray in the moonlight when the little party made their start down the long trail. Their preparations, simple and crude as they were, had taken hours of ceaseless labor on the part of the three. The ax, its edge dulled by the flame and its handle burned away, had been cooled in the snow, and with his one sound arm, Lennox had driven the hot nails that Snowbird gathered from the ashes of one of the outbuildings. The embers of the house itself still glowed red in the darkness.

Dan had cut the green limbs of the trees and planed them with his ax. The sled had been completed, handles attached for pushing it, and a piece of fence wire fastened with nails as a rope to pull it. The warm mackinaws of both of them as well as the one blanket that Lennox had saved from the fire were wrapped about the old frontiersman's wasted body,--Dan and Snowbird hoping to keep warm by the exercise of propelling the sled. Except for the dull ax and the half-empty pistol, their only equipment was a single charred pot for melting snow that Dan had recovered from the ashes of the kitchen.

The three had worked almost in silence. Words didn't help now. They wasted no sorely-needed breath. But they did have one minute of talk when they got to the top of the little ridge that had overlooked the house.

"We'll travel mostly at night," Dan told them. "We can see in the snow, and by taking our rest in the daytime, when the sun is bright and warm, we can save our strength. We won't have to keep such big fires then--and at night our exertion will keep us as warm as we can hope for. Getting up all night to cut green wood with this dull ax in the snow would break us to pieces very soon, for remember that we haven't any food. I know how; to build a fire even in the snow--especially if I can find the dead, dry heart of a rotten log-- but it isn't any fun to keep it going with green wood. We don't want to have to spend any more of our strength stripping off wet bark and hacking at sapplings than we can help; and that means we'd better do our resting in the heat of the day. After all, it's a fight against starvation more than anything else."

"Just think," the girl told them, reproaching herself, "if I'd just shot straight at that wolf to-day, we could have gone back and got his body. It might have carried us through."

Neither of the others as much as looked surprised at these amazing regrets over the lost, unsavory flesh of a wolf. They were up against realities, and they didn't mince words. Dan smiled at her gently, and his great shoulder leaned against the traces.

They moved through a dead world. The ever-present manifestations of wild life that had been such a delight to Dan in the summer and fall were quite lacking now. The snow was trackless. Once they thought they saw a snowshoe rabbit, a strange shadow on the snow, but he was too far away for Snowbird to risk a pistol shot. The pound or two of flesh would be sorely needed before the journey was over, but the pistol cartridges might be needed still more. She didn't let her mind rest on certain possibilities wherein they might be needed. Such thoughts stole the courage from the spirit, and courage was essential beyond all things else to bring them through.

Once a flock of wild geese, stragglers from the main army of waterfowl, passed overhead on their southern migration. They were many months too late. They called down their eerie cries,--that song that they had learned from the noise the wind makes, blowing over the bleak marshes. It wailed down to them a long time after the flock was hidden by the distant tree tops, and seemed to shiver, with curious echoes, among the pines. Trudging on, they listened to its last note. And possibly they understood the cry as never before. It was one of the untamed, primitive voices of the wilderness, and they could realize something of its sadness, its infinite yearning and complaint. They knew the wilderness now, just as the geese themselves did. They knew its cold, its hunger, its remorselessness, and beyond all, the fear that was bright eyes in the darkness. No man could have crossed that first twenty miles with them and remained a tenderfoot. The wild was sending home its lessons, one after another, until the spirit broke beneath them. It was showing its teeth. It was reminding them, very clearly, that in spite of houses built on the ridges and cattle pens and rifles and all the tools and aids of civilization, it was still unconquered.

Mostly the forest was heavily laden with silence. And silence, in this case, didn't seem to be merely an absence of sound. It seemed like a substance in itself, something that lay over the snow, in which all sound was immediately smothered and extinguished. They heard their own footfalls in the snow and the crunch of the sled. But the sound only went a little way. Once in a long time distant trees cracked in the frost; and they all stood still a moment, trying to fight down the vain hope that this might be some hunter from the valleys who would come to their aid. A few times they heard the snow sliding, with the dull sound of rolling window shade, down from the overburdened limbs. The trees were inert with their load of snow.

As the dawn came out, they all stood still and listened to the wolf pack, singing on the ridge somewhere behind them. It was a large pack. They couldn't make out individual voices,--neither the more shrill cry of the females, the yapping of the cubs, or the low, clear G-below-middle-C note of the males.

"If they should cross our tracks--" Lennox suggested.

"No use worrying about that now--not until we come to it," Dan told him.

The morning broke, the sun rose bright in a clear sky. But still they trudged on. In spite of the fact that the sled was heavy and broke through the snow crust as they tugged at it, they had made good time since their departure. But now every step was a pronounced effort. It was the dreadful beginning of fatigue that only food and warmth and rest could rectify.

"We'll rest now," Dan told them at ten o'clock. "The sun is warm enough so that we won't need much of a fire. And we'll try to get five hours' sleep."

"Too long, if we're going to make it out," Lennox objected.

"That leaves a work-day of nineteen hours," Dan persisted. "Not any too little. Five hours it will be."

He found where the snow had drifted against a great, dead log, leaving the white covering only a foot in depth on the lee side. He began to scrape the snow away, then hacked at the log with his ax until he had procured a piece of comparatively dry wood from its center. They all stood breathless while he lighted the little pile of kindling and heaped it with green wood,--the only wood procurable. But it didn't burn freely. It smoked fitfully, threatening to die out, and emitting very little heat.

But they didn't particularly care. The sun was warm above, as always in the mountain winters of Southern Oregon. Snowbird and Dan cleared spaces beside the fire and slept. Lennox, who had rested on the journey, lay on his sled and with his uninjured arm tried to hack enough wood from the saplings that Dan had cut to keep the fire burning.

At three they got up, still tired and aching in their bones from exposure. Twenty-four hours had passed since they had tasted food, and their unreplenished systems complained. There is no better engine in the wide world than the human body. It will stand more neglect and abuse than the finest steel motors ever made by the hands of European craftsmen. A man may fast many days if he lies quietly in one place and keeps warm. But fasting is a deadly proposition while pulling sledges over the snow.

Dan was less hopeful now. His face told what his words did not. The lines cleft deeper about his lips and eyes; and Snowbird's heart ached when he tried to encourage her with a smile. It was a wan, strange smile that couldn't quite hide the first sickness of despair.

The shadows quickly lengthened--simply leaping over the snow from the fast-falling sim. Soon it dropped down behind the ridge; and the gray of twilight began to deepen among the more distant trees. It blurred the outline and dulled the sight. With the twilight came the cold, first crisp, then bitter and penetrating to the vitals. The twilight deepened, the snow turned gray, and then, in a vague way, the fourney began to partake of a quality of unreality. It was not that the cold and the snow and their hunger were not entirely real, or that the wilderness was no longer naked to their eyes. It was just that their whole effort seemed like some dreadful, emburdened journey in a dream--a stumbling advance under difficulties too many and real to be true.

The first sign was the far-off cry of the wolf pack. It was very faint, simply a stir in the ear drums, yet it was entirely clear. That clear, cold mountain air was a perfect telephone system, conveying a message distinctly, no matter how faintly. There were no tall buildings or cities to disturb the ether waves. And all three of them knew at the same instant it was not exactly the cry they had heard before.

They couldn't have told just why, even if they had wished to talk about it. In some dim way, it had lost the strange quality of despair that it had held before. It was as if the pack were running with renewed life, that each wolf was calling to another with a dreadful sort of exultation. It was an excited cry too,--not the long, sad song they had learned to listen for. It sounded immediately behind them.

They couldn't help but listen. No human ears could have shut out the sound. But none of them pretended that they had heard. And this was the worst sign of all. Each one of the three was hoping against hope in his very heart; and at the same time 禄 hoping that the others did not understand.

For a long time, as the darkness deepened about them, the forests were still. Perhaps, Dan thought, he had been mistaken after all. His shoulders straightened. Then the chorus blared again.

The man looked back at the girl, smiling into her eyes. Lennox lay as if asleep, the lines of his dark face curiously prounounced. And the girl, because she was of the mountains, body and soul, answered Dan's smile. Then they knew that all of them knew the truth. Not even an inexperienced ear could have any delusions about the pack song now. It was that oldest of wilderness songs, the hunting-cry,--that frenzied song of blood-lust that the wolf pack utters when it is running on the trail of game. It had found the track of living flesh at last.

"There's no use stopping, or trying to climb a tree," Dan told them simply. "In the first place, Lennox can't do it. In the second, we've got to take a chance--for cold and hunger can get up a tree where the wolf pack can't."

He spoke wholly without emotion. Once more he tightened the traces of the sled.

"I've heard that sometimes the pack will chase a man for days without attacking/' Lennox told them. "It all depends on how long they've gone without food. Keep on and try to forget 'em. Maybe we can keep 'em bluffed."

But as the hours passed, it became increasingly difficult to forget the wolf pack. It was only a matter of turning the head and peering for an instant into the shadows to catch a glimpse of one of the creatures. Their forms, when they emerged from the shadows of the tree trunks, were entirely visible against the snow. They no longer yapped and howled. They acted very intent and stealthy. They had spread out in a great wing, slipping from shadow and shadow, and what were their mental processes no human being may even guess. It was a new game; and they seemed to be seeking the best means of attack. Their usual fear of men, always their first emotion, had given way wholly to a hunting cunning: an effort to procure their game without too great risk of their own lives. In the desperation of their hunger they could not remember such things as the fear of men. They spread out farther, and at last Dan looked up to find one of the gray beasts waiting, like a shadow himself, in the shadow of a tree not one hundred feet from the sled. Snowbird whipped out her pistol.

"Don't dare!" Dan's voice cracked out to her. He didn't speak loudly; yet the words came so sharp and commanding, so like pistol fire itself, that they penetrated into her consciousness and choked back the nervous reflexes that in an instant might have lost them one of their three precious shells. She caught herself with a sob. Dan shouted at the wolf, and it melted into the shadows.

"You won't do it again. Snowbird?" he asked her very humbly. But his meaning was clear. He was not as skilled with a pistol as she; but if her nerves were breaking, the gun must be taken from her hands. The three shells must be saved to the moment of utmost need.

"No," she told him, looking straight into his eyes. "I won't do it again."

He believed her. He knew that she spoke the truth. He met her eyes with a half smile. Then, wholly without warning. Fate played its last trump.

Again the wilderness reminded them of its might, and their brave spirits were almost broken by the utter remorselessness of the blow. The girl went on her face with a crack of wood. Her snowshoe had been cracked by her fall of the day before, when running to the fire, and whether she struck some other obstruction in the snow, or whether the cracked wood had simply given way under her weight, mattered not even enough for them to investigate. As in all great disasters, only the result remained. The result in this case was that her snowshoe, without which she could not walk at all in the snow, was irreparably broken.

VI

"Fate has stacked the cards against us," Lennox told them, after the first moment's horror from the broken snowshoe.

But no one answered him. The girl, whitefaced, kept her wide eyes on Dan. He seemed to be peering into the shadows beside the trail, as if he were watching for the gray forms that now and then glided from tree to tree. In reality, he was not looking for wolves. He was gazing down into his own soul, measuring his own spirit for the trial that lay before him.

The girl, unable to step with the broken snowshoe, rested her weight on one foot and hobbled like a bird with broken wings across to him. No sight of all this terrible fourney had been more dreadful in her father's eyes than this. It seemed to split open the strong heart of the man. She touched her hand to his arm.

"I'm sorry, Dan," she told him. "You tried so hard--"

Just one little sound broke from his throat--a strange, deep gasp that could not be suppressed. Then he caught her hand in his and kissed it,--again and again. "Do you think I care about that?" he asked her. "I only wish I could have done more--and what I have done doesn't count. Just as in my fight with Cranston, nothing counts because I didn't win. It's just fate, Snowbird. It's no one's fault, but maybe, in this world, nothing is ever any one's fault." For in the twilight of those winter woods, in the shadow of death itself, perhaps he was catching glimmerings of eternal truths that are hidden from all but the most far-seeing eyes.

"And this is the end?" she asked him. She spoke very bravely.

"No!" His hand tightened on hers. "No, so long as an ounce of strength remains. To fight--never to give up--may God give me spirit for it till I die."

And this was no idle prayer. His eyes raised to the starry sky as he spoke.

"But, son," Lennox asked him rather quietly, "what can you do? The wolves aren't going to wait a great deal longer, and we can't go on."

"There's one thing more--one more trial to make," Dan answered. "I thought about it at first, but it was too long a chance to try if there was any other way. And I suppose you thought of it too."

"Overtaking Cranston?"

"Of course. And it sounds like a crazy dream. But listen, both of you. If we have got to die, up here in the snow--and it looks like we had--what is the thing you want done worst before we go?"

Lennox's hands clasped, and he leaned forward on the sled. "Pay Cranston!" he said.

"Yes!" Dan's voice rang. "Cranston's never going to be paid unless we do it. There will be no signs of incendiarism at the house, and no proofs. They'll find our bodies in the snow, and we'll just be a mystery, with no one made to pay. The evidence in my pocket will be taken by Cranston, sometime this winter. If I don't make him pay, he never will pay. And that's one reason why I'm going to try to carry out this plan I've got.

"The second reason is that it's the one hope we have left. I take it that none of us are deceived on that point. And no man can die tamely--if he is a man-- while there's a chance. I mean a young man, like me,--not one who is old and tired. It sounds perfectly silly to talk about finding Cranston's winter quarters, and then, with my bare hands, conquering him, taking his food and his blankets and his snowshoes and his rifle to fight away these wolves, and bringing 'em back here."

"You wouldn't be barehanded," the girl reminded him. "You could have the pistol."

He didn't even seem to hear her. "I've been thinking about it. It's a long, long chance--much worse than the chance we had of getting out by straight walking. I think we could have made it, if the wolves had kept off and the snowshoe hadn't broken. It would have nearly killed us, but I believe we could have got out. That's why I didn't try this other way first. A man with his bare hands hasn't much of a chance against another with a rifle, and I don't want you to be too hopeful. And of course, the hardest problem is finding his camp.

"But I do feel sure of one thing: that he is back to his old trapping line on the North Fork--somewhere south of here--and his camp is somewhere on the river. I think he would have gone there so that he could cut off any attempt I might make to get through with those letters. My plan is to start back at an angle that will carry me between the North Fork and our old house. Somewhere in there I'll find his tracks, the tracks he made when he first came over to burn up the house. I suppose he was careful to mix 'em up after once he arrived there, but the first part of the way he likely walked straight toward the house from his camp.

Somewhere, if I go that way, I'll cross his trail--within ten miles at least. Then

I'll backtrack him to his camp."

"And never come back!" the girl cried.

"Maybe not. But at least everything that can be done will be done. Nothing will be left. No regrets. We will have made the last trial. I'm not going to waste any time, Snowbird. The sooner we get your fire built the better."

"Father and I are to stay here--?"

"What else can you do?" He went back to his traces and drew the sled one hundred yards farther. He didn't seem to see the gaunt wolf that backed off into the shadows as he approached. He refused to notice that the pack seemed to be steadily growing bolder. Human hunters usually had guns that could blast and destroy from a distance; but even an animal intelligence could perceive that these three seemed to be without this means of inflicting death. A wolf is ever so much more intelligent than a crow,--yet a crow shows little fear of an unarmed man and is wholly unapproachable by a boy with a gun. The ugly truth was simply that in their increasing madness and excitement and hunger, they were becoming less and less fearful of these three strange humans with the sled.

It was not a good place for a camp. They worked a long time before they cleared a little patch of ground of its snow mantle. Dan cut a number of saplings--laboriously with his ax--and built a fire with the comparatively dry core of a dead tree. True, it was feeble and flickering, but as good as could be hoped for, considering the difficulties under which he worked. The dead logs under the snow were soaked with water from the rains and the thaws. The green wood that he cut smoked without burning.

"No more time to be lost," Dan told Snowbird. "It lies in your hands to keep the fire burning. And don't leave the circle of the firelight without that pistol in your hand."

"You don't mean," she asked, unbelieving, "that you are going to go out there to fight Cranston--unarmed?"

"Of course, Snowbird. You must keep the pistol."

"But it means death; that's all it means. What chance would you have against a man with a rifle? And as soon as you get away from this fire, the wolves will tear you to pieces."

"And what would you and your father do, if I took it? You can't get him into a tree. You can't build a big enough fire to frighten them. Please don't even talk about this matter, Snowbird. My mind's made up. I think the pack will stay here. They usually--God knows how--know who is helpless and who isn't. Maybe with the gun, you will be able to save your lives."

"What's the chance of that?"

"You might--with one cartridge--kill one of the devils; and the others--but you know how they devour their own dead. That might break their famine enough so that they'd hold off until I can get back. That's the prize I'm playing for."

"And what if you don't get back?"

He took her hand in one of his, and with the other he caressed, for a single moment, the lovely flesh of her throat. The love he had for her spoke from his eyes,--such speech as no human vision could possibly mistake. Both of them were tingling and breathless with a great, sweet wonder.

"Never let those fangs tear that softness, while you live," he told her gently. "Never let that brave old man on the sled go to his death with the pack tearing at him. Cheat 'em, Snowbird! Beat 'em the last minute, if no other way remains! Show 'em who's boss, after all--of all this forest."

"You mean--?" Her eyes widened.

"I mean that you must only spend one of those three shells in fighting off the wolves. Save that till the moment you need it most. The other two must be saved--for something else."

She nodded, shuddering an instant at a menacing shadow that moved within sixty feet of the fire. The firelight half-blinded them, dim as it was, and they couldn't see into the darkness as well as they had before. Except for strange, blue-yellow lights, close together and two and two about the fire, they might have thought that the pack was gone.

"Then good-by, Dan!" she told him. And she stretched up her arms. "The thing I said--that day on the hillside--doesn't hold any more."

His own arms encircled her, but he made no effort to claim her lips. Lennox watched them quietly; in this moment of crisis not even pretending to look away. Dan shook his head to her entreating eyes. "It isn't just a kiss, darling," he told her soberly. "It goes deeper than that. It's a symbol. It was your word, too, and mine; and words can't be broken, things being as they are. Can't I make you understand?"

She nodded. His eyes blurred. Perhaps she didn't understand, as far as actual functioning of the brain was concerned. But she reached up to him, as women--knowing life in the concrete rather than the abstract--have always reached up to men; and she dimly caught the gleam of some eternal principle and right behind his words. This strong man of the mountains had given his word, had been witness to her own promise to him and to herself, and a law that goes down to the roots of life prevented him from claiming the kiss.

Many times, since the world was new, comfort--happiness--life itself have been contingent on the breaking of a law. Yet in spite of what seemed common sense, even though no punishment would forthcome if it were broken, the law has been kept. It was this way now. It wouldn't have been just a kiss such as boys and girls have always had in the moonlight. It meant the symbolic renunciation of the debt that Dan owed Cranston,--a debt that in his mind might possibly go unpaid, but which no weight of circumstance could make him renounce.

His longing for her lips pulled at the roots of him. But by the laws of his being he couldn't claim them until the debt incurred on the hillside, months ago, had been paid; to take them now meant to dull the fine edge of his resolve to carry the issue through to the end, to dim the star that led him, to weaken him, by bending now, for the test to come. He didn't know why. It had its font in the deep wells of the spirit. Common sense can't reveal how the holy man keeps strong the spirit by denying the flesAi. It goes too deep for that. Dan kept to his consecration.

He didy however, kiss her hands, and he kissed the tears out of her eyes. Then he turned into the darkness and broke through the ring of the wolves.

VII

Dan Failing was never more thankful for his unerring sense of direction. He struck off at a forty-five-degree angle between their late course and a direct road to the river, and he kept it as if by a surveyor's line. All the old devices of the wilderness--the ridge on ridge that looked just alike, inclines that to the casual eye looked like downward slopes, streams that vanished beneath the snow, and the snow-mist blowing across the face of the landmarks--could not avail against him.

A half dozen of the wolves followed him at first. But perhaps their fierce eyes marked his long stride and his powerful body, and decided that their better chance was with the helpless man and the girl beside the flickering fire. They turned back, one by one. Dan kept straight on and in two hours crossed Cranston's trail.

It was perfectly plain in the moonlit snow. He began to back-track. He headed down a long slope and in an hour more struck the

North Fork. He didn't doubt but that he would find Cranston in his camp, if he found the camp at all. The man had certainly returned to it immediately after setting fire to the buildings, if for no other reason than for food. It isn't well to be abroad on the wintry mountains without a supply of food; and Cranston would certainly know this fact.

Dan didn't know when a rifle bullet from some camp in the thickets would put an abrupt end to his advance. The brush grew high by the river, the elevation was considerably lower, and there might be one hundred camps out of the sight of the casual wayfarer. If Cranston should see him, mushing across the moonlit snow, it would give him the most savage joy to open fire upon him with his rifle.

Dan's advance became more cautious. He was in a notable trapping region, and he might encounter Cranston's camp at any moment. His keen eyes searched the thickets, and particularly they watched the sky line for a faint glare that might mean a camp fire. He tried to walk silently. It wasn't an easy thing to do with awkward snowshoes; but the river drowned the little noise that he made. He tried to take advantage of the shelter of the thickets and the trees. Then, at the base of a little ridge, he came to a sudden halt.

He had estimated just right. Not two hundered yards distant, a camp fire flickered and glowed in the shelter of a great log. He saw it, by the most astounding good fortune, through a little rift in the trees. Ten feet on either side, and it was obscured.

He lost no time. He did not know when the wolves about Snowbird's camp would lose the last of their cowardice. Yet he knew he must keep a tight grip on his self-control and not let the necessity of haste cost him his victory. He crept forward, step by step, placing his snowshoes with consummate care. When he was one hundred yards distant he saw that Cranston's camp was situated beside a little stream that flowed into the river and that--like the mountaineer he was--he had built a large lean-to reinforced with snowbanks. The fire burned at its opening. Cranston was not in sight; either he was absent from camp or asleep in his lean-to. The latter seemed the more likely.

Dan made a wide detour, coming in about thirty yards behind the construction. Still he moved with incredible caution. Never in his life had he possessed a greater mastery over his own nerves. His heart leaped somewhat fast in his breast; but this was the only wasted motion. It isn't easy to advance through such thickets without ever a misstep, without the rustle of a branch or the crack of a twig. Certain of the wild creatures find it easy; but men have forgotten how in too many centuries of cities and farms. It is hardly a human quality; and a spectator would have found a rather ghastly fascination in watching the lithe motions, the passionless face, the hands that didn't shake at all. But there were no spectators--unless the little band of wolves, stragglers from the pack that had gathered on the hills behind-- watched with lighted eyes.

Dan went down at full length upon the snow and softly removed his snowshoes. They would be only an impediment in the close work that was sure to follow. He slid along the snow crust, clear to the mouth of the lean-to.

The moonlight poured through and showed the interior with rather remarkable plainness. Cranston was sprawled, half-sitting, half-lying on a tree-bough pallet near the rear wall. There was not the slightest doubt of the man's wakefulness. Dan heard him stir, and once--as if at the memory of his deed of the day before

--he cursed in a savage whisper. Although he was facing the opening of the lean-to, he was wholly unaware of Dan's presence. The latter had thrust his head at the side of the opening, and it was in shadow. Cranston seemed to be watching the great, white snow fields that lay in front, and for a moment Dan was at loss to explain this seeming vigil. Then he understood. The white field before him was part of the long ridge that the three of them would pass on their way to the valleys. Cranston had evidently anticipated that the girl and the man would attempt to march out--even if he hadn't guessed they would try to take the helpless Lennox with them--and he wished to be prepared for emergencies. There might be sport to have with Dan, unarmed as he was. And his eyes were full of strange conjectures in regard to Snowbird. Both would be exhausted now and helpless--

Dan's eyes encompassed the room: the piles of provisions heaped against the wall, the snowshoes beside the pallet, but most of all he wished to locate Cranston's rifle. Success or failure hung on that. He couldn't find it at first. Then he saw the glitter of its barrel in the moonlight,--leaning against a grub-box possibly six feet from Cranston and ten from himself.

His heart leaped. The best he had hoped for--for the sake of Snowbird, not himself--was that he would be nearer to the gun than Cranston and would be able to seize it first. But conditions could be greatly worse than they were. If Cranston had actually had the weapon in his hands, the odds of battle would have been frightfully against Dan. It takes a certain length of time to seize, swing, and aim a rifle; and Dan felt that while he would be unable to reach it himself, Cranston could not procure it either, without giving Dan an opportunity to leap upon him. In all his dreams, through the months of preparation, he had pictured it thus. It was the test at last.

The gun might be loaded, and still--in these days of safety devices--unready to fire; and the loss of a fraction of a second might enable Cranston to reach his knife. Thus Dan felt justified in ignoring the gun altogether and trusting--as he had most desired--to a battle of hands. And he wanted both hands free when he made his attack.

If Dan had been erect upon his feet, his course would have been an immediate leap on the shoulders of his adversary, running the risk of Cranston reaching his hunting knife in time. But the second that he would require to get to his feet would entirely offset this advantage. Cranston could spring up too. So he did the next most disarming thing.

He sprang up and strode into the lean-to.

"Good evening, Cranston," he said pleasantly.

Cranston was also upon his feet the same instant. His instincts were entirely true. He knew if he leaped for his rifle, Dan would be upon his back in an instant, and he would have no chance to use it. His training, also, had been that of the hills, and his reflexes flung him erect upon his feet at the same instant that he saw the leap of his enemy's shadow. They brought up face to face. The rifle was now out of the running, as they were at about equal distances from it, and neither would have time to swing or aim it.

Dan's sudden appearance had been so utterly unlooked-for, that for a moment Cranston could find no answer. His eyes moved to the rifle, then to his belt where hung his hunting knife, that still lay on the pallet. "Good evening. Failing," he rephed, trying his hardest to fall into that strange spirit of nonchalance with which brave men have so often met their adversaries, and which Dan had now. "I'm surprised to see you here. What do you want?"

Dan's voice when he replied was no more warm than the snow banks that reinforced the lean-to. "I want your rifle--also your snowshoes and your supplies of food. And I think I'll take your blankets, too."

"And I suppose you mean to fight for them?" Cranston asked. His lips drew up in a smile, but there was no smile in the tone of his words.

"You're right," Dan told him, and he stepped nearer. "Not only for that, Cranston. We're face to face at last--hands to hands. I've got a knife in my pocket, but I'm not even going to bring it out. It's hands to hands--you and I--until everything's square between us."

"Perhaps you've forgotten that day on the ridge?" Cranston asked. "You haven't any woman to save you this time."

"I remember the day, and that's part of the debt. The thing you did yesterday is part of it too. It's all to be settled at last, Cranston, and I don't believe I could spare you if you went to your knees before me. You've got a clearing out by the fire--big as a prize ring. We'll go out there--side by side. And hands to hands we'll settle all these debts we have between us--with no rules of fighting and no mercy in the end!"

They measured each other with their eyes. Once more Cranston's gaze stole to his rifle, but lunging out, Dan kicked it three feet farther into the shadows of the lean-to. Dan saw the dark face drawn with passion, the hands clenching, the shoulder muscles growing into hard knots. And Cranston looked and knew that merciless vengeance--that age-old sin and Christless creed by which he lived--had followed him down and was clutching him at last.

He saw it in the position of the stalwart form before him, the clear level eyes that the moonlight made bright as steel, the hard lines, the slim, powerful hands. He could read it in the tones of the voice,--tones that he himself could not imitate or pretend. The hour had come for the settling of old debts.

He tried to curse his adversary as a weakling and a degenerate, but the obscene words he sought for would not come to his lips. Here was his fate, and because the darkness always fades before the light, and the courage of wickedness always breaks before the courage of righteousness, Cranston was afraid to look it in the face. The fear of defeat, of death, of Heaven knows what remorselessness with which this grave giant would administer justice was upon him, and his heart seemed to freeze in his breast. Cravenly he leaped for his knife on the blankets below him.

Dan was upon him before he ever reached it. He sprang as a cougar springs, incredibly fast and with shattering power. Both went down, and for a long time they writhed and struggled in each other's arms. The pine boughs rustled strangely.

The dark, gaunt hand reached in vain for the knife. Some resistless power seemed to be holding his wrist and was bending its bone as an Indian bends, a bow. Pain lashed through him.--And then this dark-hearted man, who had never known the meaning of mercy, opened his lips to scream that this terrible enemy be merciful to him.

But the words wouldn't come. A ghastly weight had come at his throat, and his tortured lungs sobbed for breath. Then, for a long time, there was a curious pounding, lashing sound in the evergreen boughs. It seemed merciless and endless.

But Dan got up at last, in a strange, heavy silence, and swiftly went to work. He took the rifle and filled it with cartridges from Cranston's belt. Then he put the remaining two boxes of shells into his shirt pocket. The supplies of food-- the sack of nutritious jerked venison like dried bark, the little package of cheese, the boxes of hardtack and one of the small sacks of prepared flour-- he tied, with a single kettle, into his heavy blankets and flung them with the rifle upon his back. Finally he took the pair of snowshoes from the floor. He worked coldly, swiftly, all the time munching at a piece of jerked venison. When he had finished he walked to the door of the lean-to.

It seemed to Dan that Cranston whispered faintly, from his unconsciousness, as he passed; but the victor did not turn to look. The snowshoes crunched away into the darkness. On the hill behind a half-dozen wolves--stragglers from the pack--frisked and leaped about in a curious way. A strange smell had reached them on the wind, and when the loud, fearful steps were out of hearing, it might pay them to creep down, one by one, and investigate its cause.

VIII

The gray circle about the fire was growing impatient. Snowbird waited to the last instant before she admitted this fact. But it is possible only so long to deny the truth of a thing that all the senses verify, and that moment for her was past.

At first the wolves had lingered in the deepest shadow and were only visible in profile against the gray snow. But as the night wore on, they became increasingly careless. They crept up to the very edge of the little circle of firelight; and when a high-leaping flame threw a gleam over them, they didn't shrink. She had only to look up to see that age-old circle of fire--bright dots, two and two--at every side.

It is an instinct in the hunting creatures to remain silent before the attack. The triumph cries come afterward. But they seemed no longer anxious about this, either. Sometimes she would hear their footfall as they leaped in the snow, and what excitement stirred them she didn't dare to think. Quite often one of them would snarl softly,--a strange sound in the darkness.

She noticed that when she went to her hands and knees, laboriously to cut a piece of the drier wood from the rain-soaked, rotted snag that was her principal supply of fuel, every wolf would leap forward, only to draw back when she stood straight again. At such times she saw them perfectly plainly,-- their gaunt bodies, their eyes lighted with the insanity of famine, their ivory fangs that glistened in the firelight. She worked desperately to keep the fire burning bright. She dared not neglect it for a moment. Except for the single pistol ball that she could afford to expend on the wolves--of the three she had--the fire was her last defense.

But it was a losing fight. The rain-soaked wood smoked without flame, the comparatively dry core with which Dan had started the fire had burned down, and the green wood, hacked with such heart-breaking difficulty from the saplings that Dan had cut, needed the most tireless attention to burn at all.

When Dan had gone, these little trees were well within the circle of the wolves. Unfortunately, the circle had drawn in past them. Nevertheless, now that the last of the drier dead wood was consumed, she shouldered her ax and walked straight toward the gray, crouching bodies in the snow. For a tragic second she thought that the nearest of them was going to stand its ground. But almost when she was in striking range, and its body was sinking to the snow in preparation for a leap, it skulked back into the shadow. Exhausted as she was, it seemed to her that she chopped endlessly to cut away one little length. The ax blade was dull, the handle awkward in her hand, she could scarcely stand on her broken snowshoes, and worse, the ice crust broke beneath her blows, burying the sapling in the snow. She noticed that every time she bent to strike a blow, the circle would plunge a step nearer her, withdrawing as she straightened again.

Books of woodcraft often describe with what ease a fire may be built and maintained in wet snow. It works fairly well in theory, but it is a heart-breaking task in practice. Under such difficulties as she worked, it became one of those dreadful undertakings that partake of a nightmare quality,--the walking of a treadmill or the sweeping of waves from the shore.

When she secured the first length, her fire was almost extinguished. It threw a faint cloud of smoke into the air, but the flame was almost gone. The darkness dropped about her, and the wolves came stealing over the snow. She worked furiously, with the strength of desperation, and little by little she won back a tiny flame.

Her nervous vitality was flowing from her in a frightful stream. Too long she had toiled without food in the constant presence of danger, and she was very near indeed to utter exhaustion. But at the same time she knew she must not faint. That was one thing she could not do,--to fall unconscious before the last of her three cartridges was expended in the right way.

Again she went forth to the sapling, and this time it seemed to her that if she simply tossed the ax through the air, she could fell one of the gray crowd. But when she stooped to pick it up--She didn't finish the thought. She turned to coax the fire. And then she leaned sobbing over the sled.

"What's the use?" she cried. "He won't come back. What's the use of fighting any more?"

"There's always use of fighting," her father told her. He seemed to speak with difficulty, and his face looked strange and white. The cold and the exposure were having their effect on his weakened system, and unconsciousness was a near shadow indeed. "But, dearest,--if I could only make you do what I want you to--"

"What?"

"You're able to climb a tree, and if you'd take these coats, you wouldn't freeze by morning. If you'd only have the strength--"

"And see you torn to pieces!"

"I'm old, dear--and very tired--and I'd crawl away into the shadows, where you couldn't see. There's no use mincing words, Snowbird. You're a brave girl--always have been since a little thing, as God is my judge--and you know we must face the truth. Better one of us die than both. And I promise--I'll never feel their fangs. And I won't take your pistol with me either."

Her thought flashed to the clasp hunting knife that he carried in his pocket. But her eyes lighted, and she bent and kissed him. And the wolves leaped forward even at this.

"We'll stay it out," she told him. "We'll fight it to the last--just as Dan would want us to do. Besides--it would only mean the same fate for me, in a little while. I couldn't cling up there forever--and Dan won't come back."

She was wholly unable to gain on the fire. Only by dint of the most heart-breaking toil was she able to secure any dry fuel for it at all. Every length of wood she cut had to be scraped of bark, and half the time the fire was only a sickly column of white smoke. It became increasingly difficult to swing the ax. The trail was almost at its end.

The after-midnight hours drew one by one across the face of the wilderness, and she thought that the deepening cold presaged dawn. Her fingers were numb. Her nerve control was breaking; she could no longer drive a straight blow with the ax. The number of the wolves seemed to be increasing: every way she looked she could see them leaping. Or was this just hysteria? Surely the battle could go on but a few moments more. The wolves themselves, sensing dawn, were losing the last of their cowardice.

Once more she went to one of the saplings, but she stumbled and almost went to her face at the first blow. It was the instant that her gray watchers had been waiting for. The wolf that stood nearest leaped--a gray streak out of the shadow--and every wolf in the pack shot forward with a yell. It was a short, expectant cry; but it chopped off short. For with a half-sob, and seemingly without mental process, she aimed her pistol and fired.

A fast-leaping wolf is one of the most difficult pistol targets that can be imagined. It bordered on the miraculous that she did not miss him altogether. Her nerves were torn, their control over her muscles largely gone. Yet the bullet coursed down through the lungs, inflicting a mortal wound.

The wolf had leaped for her throat; but he fell short. She staggered from a blow, and she heard a curious sound in the region of her hip. But she didn't know that the fangs had gone home in her soft flesh. The wolf rolled on the ground; and if her pistol had possessed the shocking power of a rifle, he would have never got up again. As it was, he shrieked once, then sped off in the darkness to die. Five or six of the nearest wolves, catching the smell of his blood, bayed and sped after him.

But the remainder of the great pack--fully fifteen of the gray, gaunt creatures--came stealing across the snow toward her. White fangs had gone home; and a new madness was in the air.

Straining into the silence, a perfectly straight line between Cranston's camp and Snowbird's, Dan Failing came mushing across the snow. His sense of direction had never been obliged to stand such a test as this before. Snowbird's fire was a single dot on a vast plateau; yet he had gone straight toward it.

He was risking everything for the sake of speed. He gave no heed to the fallen timber that might have torn the web of his snowshoes to shreds. Because he shut out all thought of it, he had no feeling of fatigue. The fight with Cranston had been a frightful strain on muscle and nerve; but he scarcely remembered it now. His whole purpose was to return to Snowbird before the wolves lost the last of their cowardice.

The jerked venison that he had munched had brought him back much of his strength. He was wholly unconscious of his heavy pack. Never did he glide so swiftly, so softly, with such unerring step; and it was nothing more or less than a perfect expression of the ironclad control that his steel nerves had over his muscles.

Then, through the silence, he heard the shout of the pack as the wolf had leaped at Snowbird. He knew what it meant. The wolves were attacking then, and a great flood of black, hating bitterness poured over him at the thought he had been too late. It had all been in vain, and before the thought could fully go home, he heard the dim, far-off crack of a pistol.

Was that the first of the three shots, the one she might expend on the wolves, or had the first two already been spent and was she taking the last gateway of escape? Perhaps even now Lennox was lying still on the sled, and she was standing before the ruin of her fire, praying that her soul might have wings. He shouted with all the power of his lungs across the snow.

But Snowbird only heard the soft glide of the wolves in the snow. The wind was blowing toward Dan; and while he had heard the loud chorus of the pack, one of the most far-carrying cries, and the penetrating crack of a pistol, she couldn't hear his answering shout. In fact, the wilderness seemed preternaturally still. All was breathless, heavy with suspense, and she stood, just as Dan had thought, between the ruin of her fire and the sled, and she looked with straight eyes to the oncoming wolves.

"Hurry, Snowbird," Lennox was whispering. "Give me the pistol--for that last work. We have only a moment more."

He looked very calm and brave, half-raised as he was on the sled, and perhaps a half-smile lingered at his bearded lips. And the bravest thing of all was that to spare her, he was willing to take the little weapon from her hand to use it in its last service. She tried to smile at him, then crept over to his side.

The strain was over. They knew what they had to face; She put the pistol in his steady hand.

His hand lowered to his side and he sat waiting. The moments passed. The wolves seemed to be waiting too, for the last flickering tongue of the little fire to die away. The last of her fuel was ignited and burning out; they were crouched and ready to spring if she should venture forth after more. The darkness closed down deeper, and at last only a column of smoke remained.

It was nothing to be afraid of. The great, gray leader of the pack, a wolf that weighed nearly one hundred pounds, began slowly and deliberately to set his muscles for the spring. It was the same as when the great bull elk comes to bay at the base of the cliffs: usually some one wolf, often the great pack leader, wishing to remind his followers of his might, or else some full-grown male proud in his strength, will attack alone. Because this was the noblest game that the pack had ever faced, the leader chose to make the first leap himself. It was true that these two had neither such razor-edged hoofs as the elk, yet they had eyes that chilled his heart when he tried to look at them. But one was lying almost prone, and the fire was out. Besides, the madness of starvation, intensified ten times by their terrible realization of the wound at her hip, was upon the pack as never before. The muscles bunched at his lean flanks.

But as Snowbird and her father gazed at him in fascinated horror, the great wolf suddenly smashed down in the snow. She was aware of its curious, utter collapse actually before the sound of the rifle shot that occasioned it had penetrated her consciousness. It was a perfect shot at long range; and for a long instant her tortured faculties refused to accept the truth.

Then the rifle spoke again, and a second wolf--a large male that crouched on the other side of the sled--fell kicking in the snow. The pack had leaped forward at the first death; but they halted at the second. And then terror came to them when the third wolf suddenly opened its savage lips and screamed in the death agony.

Up to this time, except for the report of the rifle, the attack had been made in utter silence. The reason was just that both breath and nervous force are needed to shout; and Dan Failing could afford to waste neither of these vital forces. He had dropped to his knee, and was firing again and again, his gray eyes looking clear and straight along the barrel, his fingers without jerk or tremor pressing again and again at the trigger, his hands holding the rifle as in a vice. Every nerve and muscle were completely in his command. The distance was far, yet he shot with deadly, amazing accuracy. The wolves were within a few feet of the girl, and a fraction's waver in the gun barrel might have sped his bullet toward her.

"It's Dan Failing," Lennox shouted as the fourth wolf died.

Then Snowbird snatched her pistol from her father's hand and opened fire. The two shells were no longer needed to free herself and her father from the agony of fangs. She took careful aim, and although a pistol is never as accurate or as powerful as a rifle, she killed one wolf and wounded another.

Frenzied in their savagery, three or four of the remaining wolves leaped at the body of one of the wounded; but the others scattered in all directions. Still Dan fired with the same unbelievable accuracy, and still the wolves died in the snow. The girl and the man were screaming now in the frenzied joy of deliverance. The wolves scurried frantically among the trees; and some of them unknowingly ran full in the face of their enemy, to be shot down without mercy. And few indeed were those that escaped,--to collect on a distant ridge, and, perhaps, to be haunted in dreams by a Death that came out of the shadows to blast the pack.

Again the pack-song would be despairing and strange in the winter nights,-- that age-old chant of Famine and Fear and the long war of existence with only Death and Darkness in the end. And because it is the voice of the wilderness itself, the tenderfoot that camps in the evergreen forest will listen, and his talk will die at his lips, and he will have the beginnings of knowledge. And perhaps he will wonder if God has given him the thews and fiber to meet the wilderness breast to breast as Dan had met it: to remain and to fight and to conquer. And thereby his metal will be tested in the eyes of the Red Gods.

Snowbird stood waiting in the snow, arms stretched to her forester as Dan came running through the wood. But his arms were wider yet, and she went softly into them.

"We will take it easy from now on," Dan Failing told them, after the camp was cleared of its dead and the fire was built high. "We have plenty of food; and we will travel a little while each day and make warm camps at night. We'll have friendship fires, just as sometimes we used to build on the ridge."

"But after you get down into the valleys?"

Lennox asked anxiously. "Are you and Snowbird coming up here to live?"

The silence fell over their camp; and a wounded wolf whined in the darkness. "Do you think I could leave it now?" Dan asked. By no gift of words could he have explained why; yet he knew that by token of his conquest, his spirit was wedded to the dark forests forever. "But heaven knows what I'll do for a living."

Snowbird crept near him, and her eyes shone in the bright firelight. "I've solved that," she said. "You know you studied forestry--and I told the supervisor at the station how much you knew about it. I wasn't going to tell you until--until certain things happened--and now they have happened, I can't wait another instant. He said that with a little more study you could get into the Forest Service--take an examination and become a ranger. You're a natural forester if one ever lived, and you'd love the work."

"Besides," Lennox added, "it would clip my Snowbird's wings to make her live on the plains. My big house will be rebuilt, children. There will be fires in the fireplace on the fall nights. There is no use of thinking of the plains."

"And there's going to be a smaller house--just a cottage at first--right beside it," Dan replied. He could go back to his forests, after all. He wouldn't have to throw away his birthright, fought for so hard; and it seemed to him no other occupation could offer so much as that of the forest rangers,--those silent, cool-nerved guardians of the forest and keepers of its keys.

For a long time Snowbird and he stood together at the edge of the firelight, their bodies warm from the glow, their hearts brimming with words they could not utter. Words always come hard to the mountain people. They are folk of action, and Dan, rather than to words, trusted to the yearning of his arms.

"We're made for each other, Snowbird darling," he told her breathlessly at last. "And at last I can claim what I've been waiting for all these months."

He claimed it; and in open defiance to all civil law, he collected fully one hundred times in the next few minutes. But it didn't particularly matter, and Snowbird didn't even turn her face. "Maybe you've forgotten you claimed it when you first came back too," she said.

So he had. It had completely slipped his mind, in the excitement of his fight with the wolf pack. And then while Lennox pretended to be asleep, they sat, breathless with happiness, on the edge of the sled and watched the dawn come out.

They had never seen the snow so lovely in the sunlight.

###

www.ingramcontent.com/pod-product-compliance
Lightning Source LLC
Chambersburg PA
CBHW071044290526
45795CB00004B/1309